Man, Faith and God

Terry Hayes

Copyright © 2018 Terry Hayes

All rights reserved.

ISBN-10: 197557220
ISBN-13: 978-1987557220

DEDICATION

This book is dedicated to my family and those that have took the time to teach me that God loves us all equally every day of our lives. I have had the honor to discuss with them the meaning of what God love is and what God wants me to be not only to myself but those around me. The understanding and applying the principles of faith in my life has been one of the many joys that I have had. This book is many years of labor trying to be the best person, husband, father, mentor, teacher, and friend that I could ever be, and the journey I have taken to become a man God will welcome one day into his kingdom.

CONTENTS

Dedication	iii
Introduction	vii
1. The definition of the characteristics and principles of faith	10
2. The Conception of God	22
Monotheism	22
God is the creator of the universe	33
Nature of God	37
To God alone may you offer prayer	49
Revelations	49
3. God's relationship with Man	57
4. People are born with the tendency to do good and evil	60
5. Moses and the Torah	63
6. The Origin of the Torah	64
7. Belief and the Belief in God's Law	65
8. The Law to Moses	73
9. The 13 Principles of Faith	81
10. The 13 Principles of Faith are as follows	85
11. The Enlightenment	87
12. The Reward and the Punishment	90
13 Israel Chosen for a Purpose	91
14. References	93

THERE IS ONLY ONE GOD, AND HE IS THE ONLY GOD. IT IS THE GOD OF ALL MEN, ALL WOMEN, AND ALL CHILDREN. IT IS THE GOD OF THE ENTIRE UNIVERSE, AND AS WE BELIEVE IN GOD WE SHARE IN HIS LOVE. GOD IS THE MOST HIGH, THE MOST GLORIOUS, THE EVER FORGIVING, THE EVER PROVIDING, THE EVER LIVING, THE SELF SUBSISTING BY WHOM ALL SUBSIST, THE LORD AND CHERISHER OF THE UNIVERSE, THE ULTIMATE TRUTH, THE ETERNAL, THE SUSTAINER, AND THE SOURCE OF ALL PEACE.

GOD IS EVERYTHING AND EVERYWHERE ALL THE TIME AND HE BELONGS TO ALL OF US AS WE ALL BELONG TO HIM. HE IS THE SAME GOD FOR EVERYONE WHETHER YOU BELIEVE IN HIM OR NOT. IT DOESN'T MATTER WHAT YOUR RELIGION, FOR ALL PEOPLE AND FOR ALL TIME.

AMEN

INTRODUCTION

I can only hope that this book will serve as your guide throughout a journey of discovery. As we embark on our journey, you should know that I am an irrelevant character. This story is not about me. It is about God and understanding the means to engage in a relationship with Him.

If your mind is open, and if you are willing to let go of the myths which permeate our world, you are on the cusp of engaging in life's greatest and most rewarding adventure. The universe we are going to explore is extraordinary, well beyond anything you may have imagined. And while the map to this magnificent realm has been available for a very long time, barely one in a million people have capitalized upon it. Very few individuals have gone where we are going which is to meet our God.

The Principles of Faith affirms that God's Word was as inerrant as language allows when it was revealed to Moses and to the Children of Israel and when it was scribed in Ancient Hebrew mankind's oldest existing alphabet. But God makes no claim that your human translation is inerrant because He knows with language, such a claim would be impossible. Beyond this, insuring continual inerrancy would require Him to interfere with freewill – something He will not do.

While language is mankind's most important tool, it is an imprecise one especially apart from Hebrew, the language God, Himself, authored.

Further, no language translates perfectly from one dialect to another, and the cultural baggage is almost always lost.

And while these are issues with which we will grapple, the biggest problem with translations is that there is often very little correlation between the text of the oldest manuscripts and what is printed on the pages of the most popular "bibles."

You may be of another religion that will not understand the big picture of what I mean by the peacemakers of God because I don't see it as a religion but to better treat each other as being on this planet and in this universe. You will hear me say in my book that "God has no religion!" and this is what God has said to me in my heart and mind.

Whether you better understand the teachings of your religion or what I am expressing here in my book given to me by God you will be able to say that God has touched me and asked me to express what it truly means to treat each other our fellow man, our wives, husbands, children, and family the way God treats us and love us.

As we all have cultural differences and understanding of what God is, I want to help people to understand what's important about setting the ground work to really loving each other from day one to the last day.

1. The definition of the characteristics and principles of faith

In the Judaism terms

There is no established formulation of **principles of faith** that are recognized by all branches of Judaism. Central authority in Judaism is not vested in any one person or group - although the Sanhedrin, the supreme Jewish religious court, would fulfill this role when it is re-established - but rather in Judaism's sacred writings, laws, and traditions.

The various principles of faith that have been enumerated over the centuries carry no weight other than that imparted to them by the fame and scholarship of their respective authors.

Judaism affirms the existence and uniqueness of God and stresses performance of deeds or commandments alongside adherence to a strict belief system. In contrast to traditions such as Christianity which demand a more explicit identification of God, faith in Judaism requires one to honor God through a constant struggle with God's instructions (Torahs) and the practice of their mitzvoth.

Orthodox Judaism stresses several core principles in its educational programs, most importantly a belief that there is one single, omniscient, transcendent, non-compound God, who created the universe, and continues to be concerned with its governance. Traditional Judaism maintains that God established a covenant with the Jewish people at Mount Sinai and revealed his laws and 613 commandments to them in the form of the Written and Oral Torah. In Rabbinic Judaism, the Torahs (Hebrew "Toroth") comprise both the written

Torah (Pentateuch) and a tradition of oral law, much of it later codified in sacred writings (see: Mishna, Talmud).

Traditionally, the practice of Judaism has been devoted to the study of Torah and observance of its laws and commandments. In normative Judaism, the Torah and hence Jewish law itself is unchanging, but interpretation of the law is more open. It is considered a mitzvah (commandment) to study and understand the law.

The proper counterpart for the general English term "faith" -as occurring in the expression "principles of faith"- would be the concept of *Emunah* in Judaism. While it is generally translated as *faith* or *trust* in God, the concept of Emunah can more accurately be described as "an innate conviction, a perception of truth that transcends (..) reason."

Emunah can be enhanced through wisdom, knowledge, understanding and learning of sacred Jewish writings. But Emunah is not simply based on reason, nor can it be understood as the opposite of or standing in contrast to reason.

There are several basic principles that were formulated by medieval rabbinic authorities. These are put forth as fundamental underpinnings inherent in the "acceptance and practice of Judaism."

Unlike other ancient Near Eastern gods, the Hebrew God is portrayed as unitary and solitary; consequently, the Hebrew God's principal relationships are not with other gods, but with the world, and more specifically, with the people he created. Judaism thus begins with ethical monotheism: the belief that God is one and is concerned with the actions of humankind. According to the Tanakh (Hebrew Bible), God promised Abraham to make of his offspring a great nation. Many generations later, he commanded the nation of Israel to love and worship only one God; that is, the Jewish nation is to reciprocate God's concern for the world. He also commanded the Jewish people to love one another; that is, Jews are to imitate God's love for people. These commandments are but two of a large corpus of commandments and laws that constitute this covenant, which is the substance of Judaism.

Thus, although there is an esoteric tradition in Judaism (Kabbalah), Rabbinic scholar Max Kadushin has characterized normative Judaism as "normal mysticism", because it involves everyday personal experiences of God through ways or modes that are common to all Jews. This is played out through the observance of the Halakha and given verbal expression in the Birkat Ha-Mizvot, the short blessings that are spoken every time a positive commandment is to be fulfilled.

The ordinary, familiar, everyday things and occurrences, we have constituted occasions for the experience of God. Such things as one's daily sustenance, the very day itself, are felt as manifestations of God's loving-kindness, calling for the *Berakhot. Kedushah*, holiness, which is nothing else than the imitation of God, is concerned with daily conduct, with being gracious and merciful, with keeping oneself from defilement by idolatry, adultery, and the shedding of blood. The *Birkat Ha-Mitzwot* evokes the consciousness of holiness at a rabbinic rite, but the objects employed in the majority of these rites are non-holy and of general character, while the several holy objects are non-theurgic. And not only do ordinary things and occurrences bring with them the experience of God. Everything that happens to a man evokes that experience, evil as well as good, for a *Berakah* is said also at evil tidings. Hence, although the experience of God is like none other, the *occasions* for experiencing Him, for having a consciousness of Him, are manifold, even if we consider only those that call for Berakot.

> Whereas Jewish philosophers often debate whether God is immanent or transcendent, and whether people have free will or their lives are determined, Halakha is a system through which any Jew acts to bring God into the world.
>
> Ethical monotheism is central in all sacred or normative texts of Judaism. However, monotheism has not always been followed in practice. The Jewish Bible (Tanakh) records and repeatedly condemns the widespread worship of other gods in ancient Israel. In the Greco-Roman era, many different interpretations of monotheism existed in Judaism, including the interpretations that gave rise to Christianity.
>
> Moreover, as a non-creedal religion, some have argued that Judaism does not require one to believe in God. For some, observance of Jewish law is more important than belief in God *per se*. In modern times, some liberal Jewish movements do not accept the existence of a personified deity active in history.

In the Christian terms

The book of Hebrews points out to us that there are seven foundational teachings that every Christian should know. As a matter of fact, the writer of Hebrews towards the end of chapter 5 says that these principles are considered milk. He goes on to say that seasoned, mature Christians should grow to the point where they get beyond learning and teaching these principles to partake of the strong meat of the word of God. Hebrews 6 highlights these seven principles:

Therefore, leaving the principles of the doctrine of Christ, let us go on unto perfection; not laying again the foundation of repentance from dead works, and of faith toward God, Of the doctrine of baptisms, and of laying on of hands, and of resurrection of the dead, and of eternal judgment. Hebrews 6:1-2

Principle #1: Repentance from dead works: This has to do with the doctrine that all of us have sinned and come short of the glory of God. Dead works are whatever actions or inactions a person does, whether good or bad, that do not glorify God even if they claim to. It includes the idea that all our acts of righteousness are as filthy rags in God's eyes when we do them without having Jesus Christ in our lives.

The Father has commanded all men everywhere to repent of their wicked ways.

Principle #2: Faith toward God: Believing that God has given us a way to be cleansed from our sins by his unearned favor to us through faith in the Lord Jesus Christ. We believe what the Father has testified to us about his son in the word including his virgin birth, his sinless nature, his 100% divinity clothed in 100% humanity, his death, burial, and resurrection on the third day which were the ultimate sacrifice for our sins. With the acceptance of these facts we know without this faith it is impossible to please God. Additionally, we know that all of God's promises to us are "yes" and "amen" when we are in Christ.

Principles #3 and #4: The doctrine of baptisms: The *first* baptism is the baptism of the Holy

Ghost we receive at the moment we sincerely believe in the Lord Jesus Christ. Through the Holy Spirit, we are sealed unto the day of our redemption (Ephesians 1:13; 4:30). The *second* baptism is the outward expression we participate in to show everyone what has taken place spiritually in our lives when we have received the Lord Jesus Christ. We allow ourselves to be immersed in water to symbolize that we are a new creation in Christ Jesus, that we believe our mortal bodies will one day be resurrected to immortality like Christ, and that we have the answer of a good conscience toward God (1 Peter 3:21).

Principle #5: Laying on of hands: Saints are called by God to use this practice to pronounce blessings on fellow saints, to bestow a God-given office or ministry to someone, to symbolically empower a person with a spiritual gift or gifts for carrying out a charge, to heal, and to receive an outward manifestation of the Holy Ghost. I covered this principle in detail in a previous post.

Principle #6: Resurrection of the dead: The belief that our Father in heaven has the power to raise the dead and that one day the dead in Christ will be raised to be reunited with their souls and spirits to live with the Godhead forever.

Principle #7: Eternal judgment: This is the second resurrection and judgment of those who reject the fact that Jesus is Lord. Unbelievers will be sentenced to everlasting destruction in the lake of fire where the smoke of their torment will rise forever (2 Thessalonians 1:8-9; Revelation 14:11).

It is interesting how God uses the number seven to establish his principles. Seven was used during the first week in Genesis to signify that God rested from his works, having completed them. These seven principles are the first principles that believers should understand and are the teachings that Jesus Christ promoted during his ministry. Our acceptance of them symbolize that we are complete in Christ and will enter his spiritual rest. Unfortunately, there are those who attend church that dispute some of these teachings to their own detriment and are unwittingly being used by Satan to try to weaken congregations. Some churches are stuck on teaching these principles over and over, but the Father wants us to grow past these baby teachings to move on to the deeper things of God.

In the Muslim terms

The **Five Pillars of Islam** "pillars of the religion") are five basic acts in Islam, considered mandatory by believers and are the foundation of Muslim life. They are summarized in the famous hadith of Gabriel.

The Shia and Sunni both agree on the essential details for the performance and practice of these acts, but the Shia do not refer to them by the same name (see Ancillaries of the Faith, for the Twelver's, and Seven pillars of Ismailism). They make up Muslim life, prayer, concern for the needy, self-purification and the pilgrimage, if one is able.

Pillars of Sunni Islam

Shahada: Faith

Shahada is a declaration of faith and trust that professes that there is only one God *(Allah)* and that Muhammad is God's messenger. It is a set statement normally recited in Arabic: *lā 'ilāha 'illā-llāhu muḥammadun rasūlu-llāh* "There is no god but God (and) Muhammad is the messenger of God." It is essential to utter it to become a Muslim and to convert to Islam.

Salat: Prayer

Salat (Ṣalāh) is the Islamic prayer. *Salat* consists of five daily prayers according to the Sunna;

the names are according to the prayer times:

Fajr (dawn), *Dhuhr* (noon), *'Aṣr* (afternoon), *Maghrib* (evening), and *'Ishā'* (night). The Fajr prayer is performed before sunrise, Dhuhr is performed in the midday after the sun has surpassed its highest point, Asr is the evening prayer before sunset, Maghrib is the evening prayer after sunset and Isha is the night prayer. All of these prayers are recited while facing in the direction of the Kaaba in Mecca and forms an important aspect of the Muslim Ummah. Muslims must wash before prayer; this washing is called *wudu* ("purification"). The prayer is accompanied by a series of set positions including; bowing with hands on knees, standing, prostrating and sitting in a special position (not on the heels, nor on the buttocks). A Muslim may perform their prayer anywhere, such as in offices, universities, and fields. However, the mosque is the more preferable place for prayers because the mosque allows for fellowship.

Zakāt: Charity

Zakāt or alms-giving is the practice of charitable giving based on accumulated wealth. The word zakāt can be defined as purification and growth because it allows an individual to achieve balance and encourages new growth. The principle of knowing that all things belong to God is essential to purification and growth. Zakāt is obligatory for all Muslims who are able to do so. It is the personal responsibility of each Muslim to ease the economic hardship of others and to strive towards eliminating inequality. Zakāt consists of spending a portion of one's wealth for the benefit of the poor or needy, like debtors or travelers. A Muslim may also donate more as an act of voluntary charity (*sadaqah*), rather than to achieve additional divine reward.

There are five principles that should be followed when giving the zakāt:

1. The giver must declare to God his intention to give the zakāt.
2. The zakāt must be paid on the day that it is due.
3. After the offering, the payer must not exaggerate on spending his money more than usual means.
4. Payment must be in kind. This means if one is wealthy then he or she needs to pay a portion of their income. If a person does not have much money, then they should compensate for it in different ways, such as good deeds and good behavior toward others.
5. The zakāt must be distributed in the community from which it was taken.

Sawm: Fasting

Three types of fasting (*Siyam*) are recognized by the Quran: Ritual fasting, fasting as compensation for repentance (both from suraAl-Baqara), and ascetic fasting (from Al-Ahzab).

Ritual fasting is an obligatory act during the month

of Ramadan. Muslims must abstain from food and drink from dawn to dusk during this month, and are to be especially mindful of other sins.[19] Fasting is necessary for every Muslim that has reached puberty (unless he/she suffers from a medical condition which prevents him/her from doing so).

The fast is meant to allow Muslims to seek nearness and to look for forgiveness from God, to express their gratitude to and dependence on him, atone for their past sins, and to remind them of the needy. During Ramadan, Muslims are also expected to put more effort into following the teachings of Islam by refraining from violence, anger, envy, greed, lust, profane language, gossip and to try to get along with fellow Muslims better. In addition, all obscene and irreligious sights and sounds are to be avoided.

Fasting during Ramadan is obligatory, but is forbidden for several groups for whom it would be very dangerous and excessively problematic. These include pre-pubescent children, those with a medical condition such as diabetes, elderly people, and pregnant or breastfeeding women. Observing fasts is not permitted for menstruating women. Other individuals for whom it is considered acceptable not to fast are those who are ill or traveling. Missing fasts usually must be made up for soon afterward, although the exact requirements vary according to circumstance.

Hajj: Pilgrimage to Mecca

The *Hajj* is a pilgrimage that occurs during the Islamic month of Dhu al-Hijjah to the holy city of Mecca. Every able-bodied Muslim is obliged to make the pilgrimage to Mecca at least once in their life. When the pilgrim is around 10 km (6.2 mi) from Mecca, he/she must dress in Ihram clothing, which consists of two white sheets. Both men and women are required to make the pilgrimage to Mecca. After a Muslim makes the trip to Mecca, he/she is known as a hajj/hajja (one who made the pilgrimage to Mecca). The main rituals of the Hajj include walking seven times around the Kaaba termed *Tawaf*, touching the Black Stone termed Istilam, traveling seven times between Mount Safa and Mount Marwah termed *Sa'yee*, and symbolically stoning the Devil in Mina termed Ramee.

The pilgrim, or the *haji*, is honored in the Muslim community. Islamic teachers say that the Hajj should be an expression of devotion to God, not a means to gain social standing. The believer should be self-aware and examine their intentions in performing the pilgrimage. This should lead to constant striving for self-improvement. A pilgrimage made at any time other than the Hajj season is called an *Umrah*, and while not mandatory is strongly recommended. Also, they make a pilgrimage to the holy city of Jerusalem in their alms-giving feast.

Pillars of Shia Islam

Twelver's

Twelver Shia Islam has five Usul al-Din and ten Furu al-Din, i.e., the Shia Islamic beliefs and practices. The Twelver Shia Islam Usul al-Din, equivalent to a Shia Five Pillars, are all beliefs considered foundational to Islam, and thus classified a bit differently from those listed above. They are:

1. *Tawhid* (Monotheism: belief in the Oneness of God)
2. *'Adl* (Divine Justice: belief in the Almighty's justice)
3. *Nubuwwah* (Prophethood)
4. *Imamah* (Succession to the Muhammad)

5. *Mi'ad* (The Day of Judgment and the Resurrection)

In addition to these Five Pillars, there are ten practices that Shia Muslims must perform, called the *Ancillaries of the Faith* (Arabic: **furū˓ al-dīn**).

1. Salat
2. Sawm
3. Zakāt, similar to Sunni Islam, it applies to money, cattle, silver, gold, dates, raisins, wheat, and barley.
4. Khums: an annual taxation of one-fifth (20%) of the gains that a year has been passed on without using. Khums is paid to the Imams; indirectly to poor and needy people.
5. Hajj
6. Jihad
7. Amr-bil-Maroof: enjoining what is right.
8. Nahi Anil Munkar: forbidding what is wrong.
9. Tawalla: expressing love towards Good.
10. Tabarra: expressing disassociation and hatred towards Evil.

Ismailis

Ismailis have their own pillars which are as follows:

- Walayah (lit. "Guardianship") denotes love and devotion to God, the prophets, the Imamah and the du˓āt ("missionaries").
- Tawhid, "Oneness of God".
- Salat: Unlike Sunni and Twelver Muslims, Nizari Ismailis reason that it is up to the current imām to designate the style and form of prayer.

- Zakāt: with the exception of the Druze, all Ismaili madh'hab have practices resembling that of Sunni and Twelver Muslims with the addition of the characteristic Shia khums.
- Sawm: Nizari and Mustaali believe in both a metaphorical and literal meaning of fasting.
- Hajj: For Ismailis, this means visiting the imām or his representative and that this is the greatest and most spiritual of all pilgrimages. The Mustaali maintain also the practice of going to Mecca. The Druze interpret this completely metaphorically as "fleeing from devils and oppressors" and rarely go to Mecca.
- Jihad or "Struggle": "the Greater Struggle" and the "The Lesser Struggle".

The Conception of God

Monotheism

Monotheism is defined by the *Encyclopedia Britannica* as belief in the existence of one god or in the oneness of God. The *Oxford Dictionary of the Christian Church* gives a more restricted definition: "belief in one personal and transcendent God", as opposed to polytheism and pantheism. A distinction may be made between exclusive monotheism, and both inclusive monotheism and pluriform monotheism which, while recognizing many distinct gods, postulate some underlying unity.

The word *monotheism* comes from the Greek meaning "single" and meaning "god". The English term was first used by Henry More(1614–1687).

In Zoroastrianism, Ahura Mazda appears as a supreme and transcendental deity. Depending on the date of Zoroaster (usually considered to be contemporary with the Vedas), this may be one of the earliest documented instances of the emergence of monism in an Indo-European religion.

Monolatrism can be a stage in the development of monotheism from polytheism. Three examples of this are the Aten cult in the reign of the Egyptian pharaoh Akhenaten, the rise of Marduk from the tutelary of Babylon to the claim of universal supremacy, and the rise of Yahweh from among the Canaanite gods to the sole God of Judaism. Ethical monotheism and the associated concept of absolute good and evil emerge in Zoroastrianism and Judaism, later culminating in the doctrines of Christology in early Christianity and later (by the 7th century) in the *tawhid* in Islam.

In the cities of the Ancient Near East, each city had a local patron deity, such as Shamash at Larsa or Sin at Ur.

The first claims of global supremacy of a specific god date to the Late Bronze Age, with Akhenaten's *Great Hymn to the Aten* (speculatively connected to Judaism by Sigmund Freud in his *Moses and Monotheism*). However, the historicity of the Exodus is disputed. Furthermore, it is not clear to what extent Akhenaten's Atenism was monotheistic rather than henotheistic with Akhenaten himself identified with the god Aten.

Currents of monism or monotheism emerge in Vedic India earlier, chiefly with worship of Lord Krishna, which is full-fledged monotheism, but also with e.g. the Nasadiya Sukta. In the Indo-Iranian tradition, the Rigveda exhibits notions of monism, in particular in the comparatively late tenth book, also dated to the early Iron Age, e.g. in the Nasadiya sukta.

According to Christian tradition, monotheism was the original religion of humanity but was generally lost after the fall of man. This theory was largely abandoned in the 19th century in favor of an evolutionary progression from animism via polytheism to monotheism, but by 1974 this theory was less widely held. Austrian anthropologist Wilhelm Schmidt had postulated an *Urmonotheismus*, "original" or "primitive monotheism" in the 1910s. It was objected that Judaism, Christianity, and Islam had grown up in opposition to polytheism as had Greek philosophical monotheism. Furthermore, while belief in a "high god" is not universal, it is found in many parts of Africa and numerous other areas of the world.

- Deism posits the existence of a single creator god, who has little or no continued involvement with the world. Samuel Clarke distinguished four types of deist: those who believed in a creator with no further interest in the world; those who also saw a certain providential ordering of the material universe but not in the moral and spiritual spheres; those who in addition, believed God had some moral attributes but did not believe in a future life; and those who, while rejecting revelation, accepted all the truths of natural religion.
- The term Henotheism has two distinct uses. In the context of biblical studies, it normally means the exclusive worship of a tribal-national deity which does not deny the reality of patron deities of other peoples, while elsewhere it often becomes a synonym for Monolatrism, that is belief in or the worship of one god without denying the existence of others. Hinduism is sometimes overgeneralized to as henotheistic.

- Monism is the philosophical stance that explains all that is in terms of a single reality and thus conflicts with any belief which distinguishes radically between different grades of being (e.g. Christianity). The type of monotheism found in Hinduism, encompassing pantheism and pantheism is monistic.
- Pantheism is a form of monistic monotheism which holds that the being of God includes and penetrates all the Universe but unlike pantheism (see below) the universe is not identical with God.
- Pantheism holds that the universe and God are identical. Philosophically, it maintains that there is only one substance which is absolute, eternal and infinite so all things, including human beings, are not independent substances but only modes or manifestations of the Absolute. The existence of a transcendent being extraneous to nature is denied.
- Substance monotheism, found in some indigenous African religions, holds that the many gods are different forms of a single underlying substance.
- Trinitarian monotheism is the Christian doctrine of belief in one God who is three distinct "persons": God the Father, God the Son (Jesus) and God the Holy Spirit. When used in this context, the word "person" is a technical term and means "something very different from what it does in common speech". In particular, the idea of self-consciousness found in contemporary usage was not at all prominent.

Judaism

God in Judaism is strictly monotheistic, an absolute one, indivisible, and incomparable being who is the ultimate cause of all existence. The Hebrew Bible presents the God of Israel as the creator of the world and as the only power controlling history. The Babylonian Talmud references other, "foreign gods" as non-existent entities to whom humans mistakenly ascribe reality and power.

The Hebrew Bible commands the Israelites not to worship other gods, but only YHWH, the God who brought them out of Egypt (Ex. 20:1-4; Deut. 5:6-7). Despite this, it records that many Israelites were rebellious, choosing instead to worship foreign gods and idols.

During the 8th century BCE, the monotheistic worship of YHWH in Israel was in competition with many other cults, described by the Yahwist faction collectively as Baals. The oldest books of the Hebrew Bible reflect this competition, as in the books of Hosea and Nahum, whose authors lament the "apostasy" of the people of Israel, threatening them with the wrath of God if they do not give up their polytheistic cults.

Some scholars hypothesize that Judaism was originally a form of Monolatrism or henotheism. In this hypothesis both the Kingdom of Israel and the Kingdom of Judah had YHWH as their state god, while also acknowledging the existence of other gods. In the 8th century BCE Assyrian royal propaganda claimed for the Assyrian national god Ashur dominion over all other gods. It is posited that in reaction to this, certain circles in Israel stressed the unique power of YHWH as a sign of national independence. The hypothesis posits a next stage, beginning with the fall of Judah to Babylon, when a small circle of priests and scribes gathered around the exiled royal court developed the first idea of YHWH as the sole God of the world.

As they traditionally profess a concept of monotheism with

a singular God, Judaism and Islam reject the Christian idea of monotheism. Judaism uses the term *shituf* to refer to ways of worshiping God not believed to be monotheistic. Muslims reject the Christian doctrine of the Trinity and divinity of Jesus, considering it to be polytheism.

The Shema

Judaism's earliest history, beliefs, laws, and practices are preserved and taught in the Torah (the first part of the Hebrew Bible). It provides a clear textual source for the rise and development of what is named Judaism's ethical monotheism which means that:

> *(1) There is one God from whom emanates one morality for all humanity. (2) God's primary demand of people is that they act decently toward one another...The God of ethical monotheism is the God first revealed to the world according to the Jewish Bible.*
> *...in the study of Hebrew history: Israel's monotheism was an ethical monotheism.* Dennis Prager

> When Moses returned with the Ten Commandments, the second of those stated that "you shall have no other gods before me" (Exodus 20:3), right after the first, which affirmed the existence of God. Furthermore, Israelites recite the Shema Israel ("Hear, O Israel") which partly says, "Hear, O Israel: YHWH is our God, YHWH is one", meaning that Israel was to worship none of the gods of other peoples. Monotheism was and is the central tenet of the Israelite and the Jewish religion.

Christianity

From earlier than the times of the Nicene Creed, 325 CE, various Christian figures advocated the triune mystery-nature of God as a normative profession of faith. According to Roger E. Olson and Christopher Hall, through prayer, meditation, study and practice, the Christian community concluded "that God must exist as both a unity and trinity", codifying this in ecumenical council at the end of the 4th century.

Christians have held that in scriptural references to 'God the Father' (Philippians 1:2, 1 Peter 1:2) 'God the Son' (John1:1, 1:14,Hebrews 1:8, Colossians Col 2:9) and 'God the Holy Spirit' (Acts 5:3-4) are referring to or describing the different divine persons. But they also still believe that passages of the New Testament, such as 1 Corinthians 8:4-6 "there is none other God but one... to us there is but one God, the Father, of whom are all things, and we in him; and one Lord Jesus Christ, by whom are all things, and we by him" and the Old Testament, such as Isaiah 45:5-7 "I am the Lord, and there is none else, there is no God beside me... there is none beside me. I am the Lord, and there is none else", claim God as being 'one'.

Many modern Christians believe the Godhead is triune meaning that the three persons of the Trinity are in one union in which each person is also wholly God. They also hold to the doctrine of a man-god Christ Jesus as God incarnate. These Christians also do not believe that one of the three divine figures is God alone and the other two are not but that all three are mysteriously God and one.

Other Christian religions including Unitarian Universalism, Jehovah's Witnesses, Mormonism and others do not share those views on the Trinity.

Historically, most Christian churches have taught that the nature of God is a *mystery*, in the original, technical meaning; something that must be revealed by special revelation rather than deduced through general revelation. Among early Christians there was considerable debate over the nature of the Godhead, with some denying the incarnation but not the deity of Jesus (Docetism) and others later calling for an Arian conception of God.

Despite at least one earlier local synod rejecting the claim of Arius, this Christological issue was to be one of the items addressed at the First Council of Nicaea.

However, some Christian faiths such as Mormonism argue that the Godhead is in fact three separate individuals which include God the Father, His Son Jesus Christ, and the Holy Ghost. Each individual having a distinct purpose in the grand existence of human kind. Furthermore, Mormons believe that before the "Council of Nicaea," the predominant belief among many early Christians was that the Godhead was three separate individuals. In support of this view, they cite early Christian examples of belief in subordinationism.

The First Council of Nicaea, held in Nicaea (in present-day Turkey), convoked by the Roman Emperor Constantine I in 325, was the first ecumenical council of bishops of the Roman Empire, and most significantly resulted in the first uniform Christian doctrine, called the Nicene Creed. With the creation of the creed, a precedent was established for subsequent 'general (ecumenical) councils of bishops' (synods) to create statements of belief and canons of doctrinal orthodoxy—the intent being to define a common creed for the Church and address heretical ideas.

One purpose of the council was to resolve disagreements in Alexandria over the nature of Jesus in relationship to the Father; in particular, whether Jesus was of the same as God the Father or merely of similar substance. All but two bishops took the first position; while Arius' argument failed.

Christian orthodox traditions (Eastern Orthodox, Oriental Orthodox, Roman Catholic, and most Protestants) follow this decision, which was reaffirmed in 381 at the First Council of Constantinople and reached its full development through the work of the Cappadocian Fathers. They consider God to be a triune entity, called the Trinity, comprising the three "persons" God the Father, God the Son, and God the Holy Spirit, the three of this unity are described as being "of the same substance" Christians overwhelmingly assert that monotheism is central to the Christian faith, as the Nicene Creed (and others), which gives the orthodox Christian definition of the Trinity, begins: "I believe in one God".

Deism is a philosophy of religion which arises in the Christian tradition during the Early Modern period. It postulates that there is a God who however does not intervene in human affairs.

Unitarianism is a theological movement, named for its understanding of God as one person, in direct contrast to Trinitarianism.

Islam

In Islam, Allah (God) is all-powerful and all-knowing, the creator, sustainer, ordainer and judge of the universe. God in Islam is strictly singular (tawhid) unique (wahid) and inherently One (ahad), all-merciful and omnipotent. Allah exist without place and the Qur'an states that "No vision can grasp Him, but His grasp is over all vision.

God is above all comprehension, yet is acquainted with all things" (Qur'an 6:103) Allah is the only God and the same God worshiped in Christianity and Judaism (29:46)

Islam emerged in the 7th century CE in the context of both Christianity and Judaism, with some thematic elements similar to Gnosticism. Islamic belief states that Muhammad did not bring a new religion from God, but is rather the same religion as practiced by Abraham, Moses, David, Jesus and all the other prophets of God. The assertion of Islam is that the message of God had been corrupted, distorted or lost over time and the Quran was sent to Muhammad in order to correct the lost message of the Torah, New Testament and prior scriptures from God.

The Qur'an asserts the existence of a single and absolute truth that transcends the world; a unique and indivisible being who is independent of the creation. The Qur'an rejects binary modes of thinking such as the idea of a duality of God by arguing that both good and evil generate from God's creative act. God is a universal god rather than a local, tribal or parochial one; an absolute who integrates all affirmative values and brooks no evil.

Tawhid constitutes the foremost article of the Muslim profession of faith, "There is no god but God, Muhammad is the messenger of God. To attribute divinity to a created entity is the only unpardonable sin mentioned in the Qur'an. The entirety of the Islamic teaching rests on the principle of *tawhid*.

As they traditionally profess a concept of monotheism with a singular person as God, Judaism and Islam reject the

Christian idea of monotheism. Judaism uses the term Shituf to refer to non-monotheistic ways of worshiping God. Though Muslims believe in Jesus (Isa in Arabic), they do not affirm that he was a begotten son of God. Jesus is mentioned more times in the Qur'an than Muhammad, but never in conjunction with the Christian doctrine of the Trinity (4:171) constituting this to be *shirk*, deviation from the true Abrahamic religion (2:135), and blasphemous excess in religion. (5:77).

Sabianism

According to the Quran, the Sabians were a monotheistic religious group. Some Hadiths account them as converts to Islam. However, this interpretation may be related to the fact that Quraysh polytheists used to describe anyone who converted to Islam with the word "Saba" which may either mean that this term was used for anyone who changed his religion or that they identified the message of Muhammed as a "Sabian belief". The former linguistic explanation (i.e. *saba = changed his religion*) is the one adopted by most Muslim scholars.

Sabians are often identified with Mandaeism, a small monotheistic community which lives today in Iraq and call themselves *Yahyawiya* Muslim scholars traditionally viewed them as followers of the
prophets Noah and *Yahya* (i.e. John the Baptist).

Bahá'í Faith

God in the Bahá'í Faith is taught to be a personal god, too great for humans to fully comprehend. Human primitive understanding of God is achieved through his revelations via his divine intermediary Manifestations. In the Bahá'í faith, such Christian doctrines as the Trinity are seen as compromising the Bahá'í view that God is single and has no equal. And the very existence of the Bahá'í Faith is a challenge to the Islamic doctrine of the finality of Muhammad's revelation. God in the Bahá'í Faith communicates to humanity through divine intermediaries, known as Manifestations of God. These Manifestations establish religion in the world. It is through these divine intermediaries that humans can approach God, and through them God brings divine revelation and law.

The Oneness of God is one of the core teachings of the Bahá'í Faith. The obligatory prayers in the Bahá'í Faith involve explicit monotheistic testimony. God is the imperishable, uncreated being who is the source of all existence.

He is described as "a personal God, unknowable, inaccessible, the source of all Revelation, eternal, omniscient, omnipresent and almighty". Although transcendent and inaccessible directly, his image is reflected in his creation.

The purpose of creation is for the created to have the capacity to know and love its creator. God communicates his will and purpose to humanity through intermediaries, known as Manifestations of God, who are the prophets and messengers that have founded religions from prehistoric times up to the present day.

God is the creator of the universe

A **creator deity** or **creator god** (often called **the Creator**) is a deity or god responsible for the creation of the Earth, world, (cosmos or universe). In monotheism, the single God is often also the creator. A number of monolatristic traditions separate a secondary creator from a primary transcendent being, identified as a primary creator.

Judaism

The creation narrative is made up of two stories, roughly equivalent to the two first chapters of the Book of Genesis. (There are no chapter divisions in the original Hebrew text, see Chapters and verses of the Bible.) The first account (1:1 through 2:3) employs a repetitious structure of divine fiat and fulfillment, then the statement "And there was evening and there was morning, the [x^{th}] day," for each of the six days of creation. In each of the first three days there is an act of division: day one divides the darkness from light, day two the "waters above" from the "waters below", and day three the sea from the land. In each of the next three days these divisions are populated: day four populates the darkness and light with sun, moon and stars; day five populates seas and skies with fish and fowl; and finally land-based creatures and mankind populate the land.

The two stories are complementary rather than overlapping, with the first (the Priestly story) concerned with the cosmic plan of creation, while the second (the Yahwist story) focuses on man as cultivator of his environment and as a moral agent. There are significant parallels between the two stories, but also significant differences: the second account, in contrast to the regimented seven-day scheme of Genesis 1, uses a simple flowing narrative style that proceeds from God's forming the first man through the Garden of Eden to the creation of the first woman and the institution of marriage; in contrast to the omnipotent God of Genesis 1, creating a god-like humanity, the God of Genesis 2 can fail as well as succeed; the humanity he creates is not god-like, but is punished for acts which would lead to their becoming god-like (Genesis 3:1-24); and the order and method of creation itself differs.[20] "Together, this combination of parallel character and contrasting profile point to the different origin of materials in Genesis 1:1 and Gen 2:4, however elegantly they have now been combined."

Christianity

Ancient Near Eastern mythologies and classical creation myths in Greek mythology envisioned the creation of the world as resulting from the actions of a god or gods upon already-existing primeval matter, known as *chaos*.

An early conflation of Greek philosophy with the narratives in the Hebrew Bible came from Philo of Alexandria (d. AD 50), writing in the context of Hellenistic Judaism. Philo equated the Hebrew creator-deity Yahweh with Aristotle's *primum movens* (First Cause) in an attempt to prove that the Jews had held monotheistic views even before the Greeks. However, this was still within the context of creation from pre-existing materials (i.e. "moving" or "changing" a material substratum.)

The classical tradition of creation from chaos first came under question in Hellenistic philosophy (on *a priori* grounds), which developed the idea that the primum movens must have created the world out of nothing.

Theologians debate whether the Bible itself teaches creation *ex nihilo*. Traditional interpreters argue on grammatical and syntactical grounds that this is the meaning of Genesis 1:1, which is commonly rendered: "In the beginning God created the heavens and the earth." They further find support for this view in New Testament passages like Hebrews 11:3—"By faith we understand that the universe was created by the word of God, so that what is seen was not made out of things that are visible"—

and Revelation 4:11—"For you [God] created all things, and by your will they existed and were created." However, other interpreters understand creation *ex nihilo* as a 2nd-century theological development. According to this view, church fathers opposed notions appearing in pre-Christian creation myths and in Gnosticism—notions of creation by a demiurge out of a primordial state of matter (known in religious studies as *chaos* after the Greek term used by Hesiod in his *Theogony*). Jewish thinkers took up the idea, which became important to Judaism, to ongoing strands in the Christian tradition, and—as a corollary—to Islam.

Islam

According to Islam, God, known in Arabic as Allah, is the all-powerful and all-knowing Creator, Sustainer, Ordainer, and Judge of the universe. Islam puts a heavy emphasis on the conceptualization of God as strictly singular (tawhid). God is unique (*wahid*) and inherently one (*ahad*), all-merciful and omnipotent. According to tradition there are 99 Names of God (al-asma al-husna lit. meaning: "The best names") each of which evoke a distinct attribute of God. All these names refer to Allah, the supreme and all-comprehensive divine name. Among the 99 names of God, the most famous and most frequent of these names are "the Compassionate" (*al-rahman*) and "the Merciful" (*al-rahim*).

Creation is seen as an act of divine choice and mercy, one with a grand purpose: "And We did not create the heaven and earth and that between them in play." Rather, the purpose of humanity is to be tested: "Who has created death and life, that He may test you which of you is best in deed. And He is the All-Mighty, the Oft-Forgiving;" Those who pass the test are rewarded with Paradise: "Verily for the Righteous there will be a fulfilment of (the heart's) desires;"

According to the Islamic teachings, God exists above the heavens and the creation itself. The Qur'an mentions, "He it is Who created for you all that is on earth. Then He Istawa (rose over) towards the heaven and made them seven heavens and He is the All-Knower of everything."[31] At the same time, God is unlike anything in creation: "There is nothing like unto Him, and He is the Hearing, the Seeing." and nobody can perceive God in totality: "Vision perceives Him not, but He perceives [all] vision; and He is the Subtle, the Acquainted." God in Islam is not only majestic and sovereign, but also a personal God: "And indeed We have created man, and We know what his own self whispers to him. And We are nearer to him than his jugular vein (by Our Knowledge)." Allah commands the believers to constantly remember Him ("O you who have believed, remember Allah with much remembrance") and to invoke Him alone ("And whoever invokes besides Allah another deity for which he has no proof - then his account is only with his Lord. Indeed, the disbelievers will not succeed.").

Islam teaches that God as referenced in the Qur'an is the only god and the same God worshipped by members of other Abrahamic religions such as Christianity and Judaism.

The Nature of God

In monotheism and henotheism, **God** is conceived of as the Supreme Being and principal object of faith.[1] The concept of God as described by theologians commonly includes the attributes of omniscience (infinite knowledge), omnipotence (unlimited power),omnipresence (present everywhere), omni

benevolence (perfect goodness), divine simplicity, and eternal and necessary existence. In theism, God is the creator and sustainer of the universe, while in deism, God is the creator, but not the sustainer, of the universe. Monotheism is the belief in the existence of one God or in the oneness of God. In pantheism, God is the universe itself. In atheism, God does not exist, while God is deemed unknown or unknowable within the context of agnosticism. God has also been conceived as
being incorporeal (immaterial), a personal being, the source of all moral obligation, and the "greatest conceivable existent". Many notable medieval philosophers and modern philosophers have developed arguments for and against the existence of God.

There are many names for God, and different names are attached to different cultural ideas about God's identity and attributes. In the ancient Egyptian era of Atenism, possibly the earliest recorded monotheistic religion, this deity was called Aten, premised on being the one "true" Supreme Being and Creator of the Universe. In the Hebrew Bible and Judaism, "He Who Is", "I Am that I Am", and the tetragrammaton YHWH are used as names of God, while Yahweh and Jehovah are sometimes used in Christianity as vocalizations of YHWH. In the Christian doctrine of the Trinity, God, consubstantial in three persons, is called the Father, the Son, and the Holy Spirit. In Judaism, it is common to refer to God by the titular names Elohim or Adonai, the latter of which is believed by some scholars to descend from the Egyptian Aten.

In Islam, the name Allah, "Al-El", or "Al-Elah" ("the God") is used, while Muslims also have a multitude of titular names for God. In Hinduism, Brahman is often considered a monistic deity. Other religions have names for God, for instance, Baha in the Baháʼí Faith,[11] Waheguru in Sikhism,[12] and Ahura Mazdain Zoroastrianism.

The many different conceptions of God, and competing claims as to God's characteristics, aims, and actions, have led to the development of ideas of omnitheism, pandeism, or a perennial philosophy, which postulates that there is one underlying theological truth, of which all religions express a partial understanding, and as to which "the devout in the various great world religions are in fact worshipping that one God, but through different, overlapping concepts or mental images of him."

Oneness

Monotheists hold that there is only one god, and may claim that the one true god is worshiped in different religions under different names. The view that all theists actually worship the same god, whether they know it or not, is especially emphasized in Hinduism and Sikhism.

In Christianity, the doctrine of the Trinity describes God as one God in three persons. The Trinity comprises God the Father, God the Son (Jesus), and God the Holy Spirit.

Islam's most fundamental concept is *tawhid* (meaning "oneness" or "uniqueness"). God is described in the Quran as: "Say: He is Allah, the One and Only; Allah, the Eternal, Absolute; He begetteth not, nor is He begotten; And there is none like unto Him." Muslims repudiate the Christian doctrine of the Trinity and divinity of Jesus, comparing it to polytheism. In Islam, God is beyond all comprehension or equal and does not resemble any of his creations in any way. Thus, Muslims are not iconodules, and are not expected to visualize God.

Theism, deism and pantheism

Theism generally holds that God exists realistically, objectively, and independently of human thought; that God created and sustains everything; that God is omnipotent and eternal; and that God is personal and interacting with the universe through, for example, religious experience and the prayers of humans. Theism holds that God is both transcendent and immanent; thus, God is simultaneously infinite and in some way present in the affairs of the world. Not all theists subscribe to all of these propositions, but each usually subscribes to some of them (see, by way of comparison, family resemblance). Catholic theology holds that God is infinitely simple and is not involuntarily subject to time. Most theists hold that God is omnipotent, omniscient, and benevolent, although this belief raises questions about God's responsibility for evil and suffering in the world. Some theists ascribe to God a self-conscious or purposeful limiting of omnipotence, omniscience, or benevolence. Open Theism, by contrast, asserts that, due to the nature of time, God's omniscience does not mean the deity can predict the future. *Theism* is sometimes used to refer in general to any belief in a god or gods, i.e., monotheism or polytheism.

Deism holds that God is wholly transcendent: God exists, but does not intervene in the world beyond what was necessary to create it. In this view, God is not anthropomorphic, and neither answers prayers nor produces miracles. Common in Deism is a belief that God has no interest in humanity and may not even be aware of humanity.

Pandeism and Panendeism, respectively, combine Deism with the Pantheistic or Panentheistic beliefs. Pandeism is proposed to explain as to Deism why God would create a universe and then abandon it, and as to Pantheism, the origin and purpose of the universe.

Pantheism holds that God is the universe and the universe is God, whereas Pantheism holds that God contains, but is not identical to, the Universe. It is also the view of the Liberal Catholic Church; Theosophy; some views of Hinduism except Vaishnavism, which believes in pantheism; Sikhism; some divisions of Neopaganism and Taoism, along with many varying denominations and individuals within denominations. Kabbalah, Jewish mysticism, paints a pantheistic/panentheistic view of God—which has wide acceptance in Hasidic Judaism, particularly from their founder The Baal Shem Tov—but only as an addition to the Jewish view of a personal god, not in the original pantheistic sense that denies or limits persona to God.

Non-theistic views of God

Even non-theist views about gods vary. Some non-theists avoid the concept of God, whilst accepting that it is significant to many; other non-theists understand God as a symbol of human values and aspirations. The nineteenth-century English atheist Charles Bradlaugh declared that he refused to say "There is no God", because "the word 'God' is to me a sound conveying no clear or distinct affirmation"; he said more specifically that he disbelieved in the Christian god. Stephen Jay Gould proposed an approach dividing the world of philosophy into what he called "non-overlapping magisteria" (NOMA). In this view, questions of the supernatural, such as those relating to the existence and nature of God, are non-empirical and are the proper domain of theology. The methods of science should then be used to answer any empirical question about the natural world, and theology should be used to answer questions about ultimate meaning and moral value. In this view, the perceived lack of any empirical footprint from the magisterium of the supernatural onto natural events makes science the sole player in the natural world.

Another view, advanced by Richard Dawkins, is that the existence of God is an empirical question, on the grounds that "a universe with a god would be a completely different kind of universe from one without, and it would be a scientific difference." Carl Sagan argued that the doctrine of a Creator of the Universe was difficult to prove or disprove and that the only conceivable scientific discovery that could disprove the existence of a Creator would be the discovery that the universe is infinitely old.[51]

Stephen Hawking and co-author Leonard Mlodinow state in their book, *The Grand Design*, that it is reasonable to ask who or what created the universe, but if the answer is God, then the question has merely been deflected to that of who created God. Both authors claim however, that it is possible to answer these questions purely within the realm of science, and without invoking any divine beings. Neuroscientist Michael Nikoletseas has proposed that questions of the existence of God are no different from questions of natural sciences. Following a biological comparative approach, he concludes that it is highly probable that God exists, and, although not visible, it is possible that we know some of his attributes.

The Essence of God

Countless arguments have been proposed in attempt to prove the existence of God. Some of the most notable arguments are the Five Ways of Aquinas, the Argument from Desire proposed by C.S. Lewis, and the Ontological

Argument formulated both by St. Anselm and René Descartes. Even among theists, these proofs are debated, and some, such as the Ontological Argument, are highly controversial.

Aquinas spends a section of his treatise on God refuting St. Anselm's proof. St. Anselm's approach was to define God as, "that than which nothing greater can be conceived". Famed pantheist philosopher Baruch Spinoza would later carry this idea to its extreme: "By God I understand a being absolutely infinite, i.e., a substance consisting of infinite attributes, of which each one expresses an eternal and infinite essence." For Spinoza, the whole of the natural universe is made of one substance, God, or its equivalent, Nature. His proof for the existence of God was a variation of the Ontological argument.

St. Thomas believed that the existence of God is self-evident in itself, but not to us. "Therefore I say that this proposition, "God exists", of itself is self-evident, for the predicate is the same as the subject.... Now because we do not know the essence of God, the proposition is not self-evident to us; but needs to be demonstrated by things that are more known to us, though less known in their nature—namely, by effects."

St. Thomas believed that the existence of God can be demonstrated. Briefly in the *Summa theologian* and more extensively in the *Summa contra Gentiles*, he considered in great detail five arguments for the existence of God, widely known as the *quinque viae* (Five Ways).

1. Motion: Some things undoubtedly move, though cannot cause their own motion. Since, as Thomas believed, there can be no infinite chain of causes of motion, there must be a First Mover not moved by

anything else, and this is what everyone understands by God.
2. Causation: As in the case of motion, nothing can cause itself, and an infinite chain of causation is impossible, so there must be a First Cause, called God.
3. Existence of necessary and the unnecessary: Our experience includes things certainly existing but apparently unnecessary. Not everything can be unnecessary, for then once there was nothing and there would still be nothing. Therefore, we are compelled to suppose something that exists necessarily, having this necessity only from itself; in fact, itself the cause for other things to exist.
4. Gradation: If we can notice a gradation in things in the sense that some things are more hot, good, etc., there must be a superlative that is the truest and noblest thing, and so most fully existing. This then, we call God -- note Thomas does not ascribe actual qualities to God Himself.
5. Ordered tendencies of nature: A direction of actions to an end is noticed in all bodies following natural laws. Anything without awareness tends to a goal under the guidance of one who is aware. This we call God -- Note that even when we guide objects, in Thomas's view the source of all our knowledge comes from God as well.

Some theologians, such as the scientist and theologian A.E. McGrath, argue that the existence of God is not a question that can be answered using the scientific method.
Agnostic Stephen Jay Gould argues that science and religion are not in conflict and do not overlap.

There are many philosophical issues concerning the

existence of God. Some definitions of God are nonspecific, while others can be self-contradictory. Arguments for the existence of God typically include metaphysical, empirical, inductive, and subjective types, while others revolve around the order and complexity in the world and perceived holes in evolutionary theory.

Arguments against the existence of God typically include empirical, deductive, and inductive types. Conclusions reached include views that: "God does not exist" (strong atheism); "God almost certainly does not exist" (*de facto* atheism); "no one knows whether God exists" (agnosticism);

"God exists, but this cannot be proven or disproven" (weak theism); and that "God exists and this can be proven" (strong theism). There are numerous variations on these positions.

God in Christianity

God in Christianity is the eternal being who created and preserves all things. Christians believe God to be both transcendent (wholly independent of, and removed from, the material universe) and immanent (involved in the world). Christian teachings of the immanence and involvement of God and his love for humanity exclude the belief that God is of the same substance as the created universe but accept that God's divine Nature was hypostatically united to human nature in the person of Jesus Christ, in an event known as the Incarnation.

Early Christian views of God were expressed in the Pauline Epistles and the early creeds, which proclaimed one God and the divinity of Jesus, almost in the same breath as in 1 Corinthians (8:5-6): "For even if there are so-called gods, whether in heaven or on earth (as indeed there are many 'gods' and many 'lords'), yet for us there is but one God, the Father, from whom all things came and for whom we live; and there is but one Lord, Jesus Christ, through whom all things came and through whom we live." "Although the Judeo-Christian sect of the Ebonite's protested against this apotheosis of Jesus, the great mass of Gentile Christians accepted it." This began to differentiate the Gentile Christian views of God from traditional Jewish teachings of the time.

The theology of the attributes and nature of God has been discussed since the earliest days of Christianity, with Irenaeus writing in the 2nd century: "His greatness lacks nothing, but contains all things". In the 8th century, John of Damascus listed eighteen attributes which remain widely accepted. As time passed, theologians developed systematic lists of these attributes, some based on statements in the Bible (e.g., the Lord's Prayer, stating that the Father is in Heaven), others based on theological reasoning. The Kingdom of God is a prominent phrase in the Synoptic Gospels and while there is near unanimous agreement among scholars that it represents a key element of the teachings of Jesus, there is little scholarly agreement on its exact interpretation.

Although the New Testament does not have a formal doctrine of the Trinity as such, it does repeatedly speak of the Father, the Son, and the Holy Spirit in such a way as to "compel a trinitarian understanding of God." This never becomes atritheism, i.e. this does not imply three Gods.[16] Around the year 200, Tertullian formulated a version of the doctrine of the Trinity which clearly affirmed the divinity of Jesus and came close to the later definitive form produced by the Ecumenical Council of 381. The doctrine of the Trinity can be summed up as: "The One God exists in Three Persons and One Substance, as God the Father, God the Son and God the Holy Spirit." Trinitarians, who form the large majority of Christians, hold it as a core tenet of their faith. Nontrinitarian denominations define the Father, the Son, and the Holy Spirit in a number of different ways.

God in Judaism

The traditional conception of **God in Judaism** is strictly monotheistic. God is generally understood by Jews to be the absolute one, indivisible and incomparable being who is the ultimate cause of all existence. Jewish tradition teaches that the true aspect of God is incomprehensible and unknowable, and that it is only God's revealed aspect that brought the universe into existence, and interacts with mankind and the world. The one God of Israel is the God of Abraham, Isaac, and Jacob, who is the guide of the world, delivered the Israelites from slavery in Egypt, and gave them the Law of Moses at biblical Mount Sinai as described in the Torah. Traditional interpretations of Judaism generally emphasize that God is personal, while some modern interpretations of Judaism emphasize that God is a force or ideal.

God has a proper name written YHWH (Hebrew: יְהֹוָה, Modern *Yehovah*, Tiberian

Yəhōwāh) in the Hebrew Bible. In Jewish tradition another name of God is Elohim.

God in Islam

In Islamic theology, **God** (Arabic: الله *Allāh*) is the all-powerful and all-knowing creator, sustainer, ordainer and judge of everything in existence. Islam emphasizes that

God is strictly singular (*tawḥīd*) unique (*wāḥid*) and inherently One (*aḥad*), all-merciful and omnipotent. According to Islamic teachings, God exists without place and according to the Quran, "No vision can grasp him, but His grasp is over all vision: He is above all comprehension, yet is acquainted with all things." God, as referenced in the Quran, is the only God.

Definition of God is given in the Surat 112 Al-'Ikhlāṣ (The Sincerity) it says "He is God, [who is] One. God, the Eternal Refuge.

He neither begets nor is born, nor is there to Him any equivalent."

In Islam, there are 99 known names of God (*al-asmā' al-ḥusná* lit. meaning: "The best names"), each of which evoke a distinct attribute of God. All these names refer to Allah, the supreme and all-comprehensive divine name. Among the 99 names of God, the most familiar and frequent of these names are "the Compassionate" (*Ar-Raḥmān*) and "the Merciful" (*Ar-Raḥīm*). Creation and ordering of the universe is seen as an act of prime mercy for which all creatures sing God's glories and bear witness to God's unity and lordship. God responds to those in need or distress whenever they call. Above all, God guides humanity to the right way, "the holy ways".

Islamic theology makes a distinction between the attributes of God and the divine essence. Islam also has a concept of negative theology, known as *ta'tili* "negation", stating that God exists without a place and has no resemblance to his creation. The former belief of God not having a place is held by fringe Islamic groups only but rejected by most mainstream Muslims.

To God alone may one offer prayer

With Christians, Judaism, and Islam there has often emphasize strict monotheism and "exclusivity of the divinity" and prayer directly to God; references to angels or other intermediaries are not typically seen in these religions or in prayer books. Principle of faith states that "I believe with perfect faith that it is only proper to pray to God," and this is often seen as stating that "One may not pray to anyone or anything else. This principle teaches that God is the only one whom we may serve and praise... It is therefore not proper to serve (angels, stars, or other elements) or make them intermediaries to bring us closer to God." Talmudic literature does shows that some evidence that Jewish prayers invoking angels and other intermediaries existed in the 1st century CE, and several examples of post-Talmudic prayers exist, including a familiar *piyyut* (liturgical song) entitled "Usherers of Mercy," recited before and after Rosh Hashanah in Selichot (Jewish penitential prayers).

Revelation

In religion and theology, **revelation** is the revealing or disclosing of some form of truth or knowledge through communication with a deity or other supernatural entity or entities.

Some religions have religious texts which they view as divinely or supernaturally revealed or inspired.

Orthodox Jews, Christians and Muslims believe that the *Torah* was received from Yahweh on biblical Mount Sinai. Most Christians believe that both the Old Testament and the New Testament were inspired by God. Muslims believe the Quran was revealed by God to Muhammad word by word through the angel Gabriel (*Jibril*). In Hinduism, some Vedas are considered *apauruṣeya*, "not human compositions", and are supposed to have been directly revealed, and thus are called *śruti*, "what is heard". The 15,000 handwritten pages produced by the mystic Maria Valtorta were represented as direct dictations from Jesus, while she attributed *The Book of Azariah* to her guardian angel. Aleister Crowley stated that *The Book of the Law* had been revealed to him through a higher being that called itself *Aiwass*.

A revelation communicated by a supernatural entity reported as being present during the event is called a vision. Direct conversations between the recipient and the supernatural entity, or physical marks such as stigmata, have been reported. In rare cases, such as that of Saint Juan Diego, physical artifacts accompany the revelation.

The Roman Catholic concept of interior locution includes just an inner voice heard by the recipient.

In the Abrahamic religions, the term is used to refer to the process by which God reveals knowledge of himself, his will, and his divine providence to the world of human beings. In secondary usage, revelation refers to the resulting human knowledge about God, prophecy, and other divine things. Revelation from a supernatural source plays a less important role in some other religious traditions such as Buddhism, Confucianism and Taoism.

Revelation may be defined as the communication of some truth by God to a rational creature through means which are beyond the ordinary course of nature. Judaism is the only religion in history that is based on a mass-revelation of God, as opposed to revelations or visions to individuals or small groups of persons or family members, i.e. Quran, Mormonism, Christianity, Buddhism, Scientology. The account of this mass-event, when a large group of people became witnesses to a revelation of Yahweh, is recorded in the parashah Yitro, the seventeenth weekly Torah portion, in the second book of the Torah.

The parashah tells of Jethro's organizational counsel to Moses and God's mass-revelation, and of the giving of the Ten Commandments to the Israelites at Mount Sinai.

Christianity

Many Christians believe in the possibility and even reality of private revelations, messages from God for individuals, which can come in a variety of ways. Montanism is an example in early Christianity and there are alleged cases today also. However, Christians see as of a much higher level the revelation recorded in the collection of books known as the Bible. They consider these books to be written by human authors under the inspiration of the Holy Spirit. They regard Jesus as the supreme revelation of God, with the Bible being a revelation in the sense of a witness to him. The *Catechism of the Catholic Church* states that "the Christian faith is not a 'religion of the book.' Christianity is the religion of the 'Word of God', a word which is 'not a written and mute word, but the Word which is incarnate and living".

Gregory and Nix speak of Biblical inerrancy as meaning that, in its original form, the Bible is totally without error, and free from all contradiction, including the historical and scientific parts. Coleman speaks of Biblical infallibility as meaning that the Bible is inerrant on issues of faith and practice but not history or science. The Catholic Church speaks not about infallibility of Scripture but about its freedom from error, holding "the doctrine of the inerrancy of Scripture". The Second Vatican Council, citing earlier declarations, stated: "Since everything asserted by the inspired authors or sacred writers must be held to be asserted by the Holy Spirit, it follows that the books of Scripture must be acknowledged as teaching solidly, faithfully and without error that truth which God wanted put into sacred writings for the sake of salvation". It added: "Since God speaks in Sacred Scripture through men in human fashion, the interpreter of Sacred Scripture, in order to see clearly what God wanted to communicate to us, should carefully investigate what meaning the sacred writers really intended, and what God wanted to manifest by means of their words." The Reformed Churches believe in the Bible is inerrant in the sense spoken of by Gregory and Nix and "deny that Biblical infallibility and inerrancy are limited to spiritual, religious, or redemptive themes, exclusive of assertions in the fields of history and science". The Westminster Confession of Faith speaks of "the infallible truth and divine authority" of the Scriptures.

In the New Testament, Jesus treats the Old Testament as authoritative and says it "cannot be broken" (John 10:34–36). 2 Timothy 3:16 says: "All Scripture is breathed out by God and profitable for teaching, for reproof, for correction, and for training in righteousness".

The Second Epistle of Peter claims that "no prophecy of Scripture comes from someone's own interpretation. For no prophecy was ever produced by the will of man, but men spoke from God as they were carried along by the Holy Spirit" (2 Peter 1:20–21). It also speaks of Paul's letters as containing some things "hard to understand, which the ignorant and unstable twist to their own destruction, as they do the other Scriptures".

This letter does not specify "the other Scriptures", nor does the term "all Scripture" in 2 Timothy indicate which writings were or would be Breathed out by God and useful for teaching, since it does not preclude later works, such as the Book of Revelation and the Epistles of John may have been. The Catholic Church recognizes 73 books as inspired and forming the Bible (56 books of the Old Testament and 27 books of the New Testament). The most common versions of the Bible that Protestants have today consist of 66 of these books. None of the 66 or 73 books gives a list of revealed books.

Theologian and Christian existentialist philosopher Paul Johannes Tillich (1886–1965), who sought to correlate culture and faith so that "faith need not be unacceptable to contemporary culture and contemporary culture need not be unacceptable to faith", argued that revelation never runs counter to reason (affirming Thomas Aquinas who said that faith is eminently rational), and that both poles of the subjective human experience are complementary.

Karl Barth argued that God is the object of God's own self-knowledge, and revelation in the Bible means the self-unveiling to humanity of the God who cannot be discovered by humanity simply through its own efforts. For him, the Bible is not *The Revelation*; rather, it points to revelation.

Human concepts can never be considered as identical to God's revelation, and Scripture is written in human language, expressing human concepts.

It cannot be considered identical with God's revelation. However, God does reveal himself through human language and concepts, and thus Christ is truly presented in scripture and the preaching of the church.

Islam

Muslims believe that God (Arabic: *Allah*) revealed his final message to humanity through Muhammad via the angel Gabriel. Muhammad is considered to have been the Seal of the Prophets and Muhammad's revelations, the Qur'an, is believed by Muslims to be the flawless final revelation of God to humanity, valid until the Last Day. The Qur'an claims to have been revealed word by word and letter by letter. Muslims hold that the message of Islam is the same as the message preached by all the messengers sent by God to humanity since Adam. Muslims believe that Islam is the oldest of the monotheistic religions because it represents both the original and the final revelation of God to Abraham, Moses, David, Jesus, and Muhammad. Likewise, Muslims believe that every prophet received revelation in their lives, as each prophet was sent by God to guide mankind. Jesus is significant in this aspect as he received revelation in a twofold aspect, as Muslims believe he preached the Gospel while also having been taught the Torah.

According to Islamic traditions, Muhammad began receiving revelations from the age of 40, delivered through the angel Gabriel over the last 23 years of his life. The content of these revelations, known as the Qur'an, was memorized and recorded by his followers and compiled from dozens of hafiz as well as other various parchments or hides into a single volume shortly after his death. In Muslim theology, Muhammad is considered equal in importance to all other prophets of God and to make distinction among the prophets is as in, as the Qur'an itself promulgates equality between God's prophets. (Qur'an 3:84)

Many scholars have made the distinction between revelation and inspiration, which according to Muslim theology, all righteous people can receive. Inspiration refers to God inspiring a person to commit some action, as opposed to revelation, which only the prophets received. Moses's mother, Jochebed, being inspired to send the infant Moses in a cradle down the Nile river is a frequently cited example of inspiration, as is Hagar searching for water for the infant Ishmael.

Judaism

The term "revelation" is used in two senses in Jewish theology; it either denotes (1) what in rabbinical language is called "Gilluy Shekinah," a manifestation of God by some wondrous act of His which overawes man and impresses him with what he sees, hears, or otherwise perceives of His glorious presence; or it denotes (2) a manifestation of His will through oracular words, signs, statutes, or laws.

In Judaism, issues of epistemology have been addressed by Jewish philosophers such as Saadiah Gaon (882–942) in his Book of Beliefs and Opinions; Maimonides (1135–1204) in his Guide for the Perplexed; Samuel Hugo Berman, professor of philosophy at the Hebrew University; Joseph Dov Soloveitchik (1903–1993), talmudic scholar and philosopher; Neil Gillman, professor of philosophy at the Jewish Theological Seminary of America, and Elliot N. Dorff, professor of philosophy at the American Jewish University.

One of the major trends in modern Jewish philosophy was the attempt to develop a theory of Judaism through existentialism. One of the primary players in this field was Franz Rosenzweig. His major work, *Star of Redemption*, expounds a philosophy in which he portrays the relationships between God, humanity and world as they are connected by creation, revelation and redemption. Conservative Jewish philosophers Elliot N. Dorff and Neil Gillman take the existentialist philosophy of Rosenzweig as one of their starting points for understanding Jewish philosophy. (They come to different conclusions, however.)

Rabbinic Judaism, and contemporary Orthodox Judaism, hold that the Torah (Pentateuch) extant today is essentially the same one that the whole of the Jewish people received on Mount Sinai, from God, upon their Exodus from Egypt. Beliefs that God gave a "Torah of truth" to Moses (and the rest of the people), that Moses was the greatest of the prophets, and that the Law given to Moses will never be changed, are three of the Thirteen Principles of Faith of Orthodox Judaism according to Maimonides. Maimonides explains: "We do not know exactly how the Torah was transmitted to Moses. But when it was transmitted, *Moses merely wrote it down like a secretary taking dictation...*(Thus) *every verse in the Torah is equally holy, as they all originate from God*, and are all part of God's Torah, which is perfect, holy and true."

Orthodox Judaism believes that in addition to the written Torah, God also revealed to Moses a set of oral teachings, called the Oral Torah. In addition to this revealed law, Jewish law contains decrees and enactments made by prophets, rabbis, and sages over the course of Jewish history. Haredi Judaism tends to regard even rabbinic decrees as being of divine origin or divinely inspired, while Modern Orthodox Judaism tends to regard them as being more potentially subject to human error, although due to the Biblical verse "Do not stray from their words" ("Deuteronomy 17:11) it is still accepted as binding law.

Conservative Judaism tends to regard both the Torah and the Oral law as not verbally revealed. The Conservative approach tends to regard the Torah as compiled by redactors in a manner similar to the Documentary Hypothesis. However, Conservative Jews also regard the authors of the Torah as divinely inspired, and many regard at least portions of it as originating with Moses. Positions can vary from the position of Joel Roth, following David Weiss HaLivni, that while the Torah originally given to Moses on Mount Sinai became corrupted or lost and had to be recompiled later by redactors, the recompiled Torah is nonetheless regarded as fully Divine and legally authoritative, to the position of Gordon Tucker that the Torah, while Divinely inspired, is a largely human document containing significant elements of human error, and should be regarded as the beginning of an ongoing process which is continuing today. Conservative Judaism regards the Oral Law as divinely inspired, but nonetheless subject to human error.

Reform and Reconstructionist Jews also accept the Documentary Hypothesis for the origin of the Torah, and tend to view all of the Oral law as an entirely human creation. Reform believe that the Torah is not a direct revelation from God, but is a document written by human ancestors, carrying human understanding and experience, and seeking to answer the question: 'What does God require of us?'. They believe that, though it contains many 'core-truths' about God and humanity, it is also time bound. They believe that God's will is revealed through the interaction of humanity and God throughout history, and so, in that sense, Torah is a product of an ongoing revelation. Reconstructionist Judaism denies the notion of revelation entirely.

God's Relationship with Man

Some have classified God's relationship with man in the

Bible according to the following considerations: 1) God, 2) men in general, that is, humanity in general, 3) the individual, 4) the God-man, 5) God and man, 6) God in man, and 7) God over men. This is a good division. First, we have God; this is clear enough. Second, we have all men, that is, humanity. This includes Adam's fall and sin and everything that is in Adam. Third, we have the individual, which includes individual sin and individual judgment. Fourth, we have the God-man, which we see in the Gospels; the Lord Jesus is the God-man. Fifth, we have God and man, which involves the truth of the gospel preached in the Epistles. Sixth, we have God in man, which points to all of God's operations within man, involving the deeper truths in the Epistles. Seventh, we have God over men, which refers the kingdom age, when God will be King over all men. This includes all future events. We can adopt this plan and write down all the subjects in seven different notebooks.

The study of biblical chronology may not reap much immediate benefit. But at least it will help the reader to develop a careful habit in reading the Word. The Bible contains clear records of chronology. One can calculate the exact number of years from man's creation to the birth of Jesus. From Adam to the flood is clearly 1,656 years. The Bible clearly gives us a record of the number of years for each period of history. Thus, we know the number of years from the time of the exodus to the entrance into Canaan. We know the number of years the Israelites lived under the judges, the number of years they lived under the kings, and the number of years from that time until the time of Daniel and from then to the time of the Lord Jesus. Some numbers are found in Stephen's words. We even find a record of the number of years a certain person slept on his right and the number of years he slept on his left (Ezek. 4:4-6). From the time of the rebuilding of Jerusalem to the coming of the Lord Jesus was sixty-nine weeks (483 years). In this way, we can trace the number of years all the way from Adam to the Lord Jesus. Beginning from Genesis God has laid down a chronology, and this chronology has never been interrupted. In order to study the Bible, we have to learn to be a careful and attentive person.

In studying chronology, we can discover things we ordinarily would not discover. For example, when we study the history of the patriarchs, we find that Adam was still alive at the time Enoch was walking on the earth. Adam had seen God, but Enoch had never seen God. We may think that the one who had seen God should have been raptured. But in the end Enoch was raptured; Adam was not raptured. This is a lesson to us. Further along we find the name Methuselah, which means "when he dies, something will happen." In the year that Methuselah died, the flood came. This also shows the accuracy of the Bible.

Paul tells us in Galatians 3 that grace preceded the law; it did not come after the law. We have to know the chronology, and then we will see that the grace of promise was in existence 430 years before the coming of the law.

It is easy to find biblical chronology from the book of Genesis. After Genesis it is more difficult to dig out the chronology. Yet the difficulty lies only in man's reluctance to study the Word. How many years are there from Israel's exodus out of Egypt to Solomon's building of the temple? First Kings 6:1 says, "Then in the four hundred eightieth year after the children of Israel had come forth out of the land of Egypt, in the fourth year of his reign over Israel, in the month of Ziv (this is the second month), Solomon began to build the house of Jehovah." Yet Acts 13:18-22 says, "And for a time of about forty years He carried them as a nurse in the wilderness.…And after these things, for about four hundred and fifty years, He gave them judges until Samuel the prophet. And afterward…God gave them Saul…for forty years. And when He had deposed him, He raised up David for them as king." All these years added together equal 530 years. When David's reign of forty years (1 Kings 2:11) and the three years of Solomon's reign before he built the temple are also added, the number of years comes to 573. Hence the record of 1 Kings has ninety-three fewer years than the record of Acts 13. What is the reason for this difference? According to the record of Judges, the children of Israel were taken captive five times. The first lasted eight years (3:8), the second eighteen years (v. 14), the third twenty years (4:2-3), the fourth seven years (6:1), and the last forty years (13:1). All of these years added together equal exactly ninety-three years. It seems that 1 Kings is short of ninety-three years. Actually, it purposely deleted the years of captivity. There is a need of the supplement of the record of Judges. The records of the Bible are like a chain; no link in the chain can be missing. Every link has to be present. God Himself has put these together, and all we have to do is find the links.

Hence, the study of chronology is very useful in training us to be accurate.

Judaism's focus is more on how God defines man than one trying to define God. There is therefore a focus on what people are expected to be or do far more than on spelling out theological beliefs.

People are born with both a tendency to do good and

to do evil

Jewish tradition mostly emphasizes free will, and most Jewish thinkers reject determinism, on the basis that free will and the exercise of free choice have been considered a precondition of moral life. "Moral indeterminacy seems to be assumed both by the Bible, which bids man to choose between good and evil, and by the rabbis, who hold the decision for following the good inclination rather than the evil rests with every individual." Maimonides asserted the compatibility of free will with foreknowledge of God (Mishneh Torah, Hilkhot Teshuvah 5). Only a handful of Jewish thinkers have expressed deterministic views. This group includes the medieval Jewish philosopher Hasdai Crescas and the 19th-century Hasidic rabbi Mordechai Yosef Leiner of Izbica.

Judaism affirms that people are born with both an *yetzer ha-tov*, an inclination or impulse to do good, and with a *yetzer hara*, an inclination or impulse to do evil. These phrases reflect the concept that "within each person, there are opposing natures continually in conflict" and are referenced many times in the rabbinic tradition. The rabbis even recognize a positive value to the *yetzer ha-ra*: without the *yetzer ha-ra* there would be no civilization or other fruits of human labor. Midrash (Bereshit Rabbah 9:7) states: "Without the evil inclination, no one would father a child, build a house, or make a career." The implication is that *yetzer ha-tov* and *yetzer ha-ra* are best understood not only as moral categories of good and evil but as the inherent conflict within man between selfless and selfish orientations.

Judaism recognizes two classes of "sin": offenses against other people, and offenses against God. Offenses against God may be understood as violation of a contract (the covenant between God and the Children of Israel).

A classical rabbinic work, *Avoth de-Rabbi Natan*, states: "One time, when Rabban Yochanan ben Zakkai was walking in Jerusalem with Rabbi Yehosua, they arrived at where the Temple in Jerusalem now stood in ruins. "Woe to us," cried Rabbi Yehosua, "for this house where atonement was made for Israel's sins now lies in ruins!" Answered Rabban Yochanan, "We have another, equally important source of atonement, the practice of *gemiluth ḥasadim* (loving kindness), as it is stated: "I desire loving kindness and not sacrifice" (Hosea 6:6). Also, the Babylonian Talmud teaches that "Rabbi Yochanan and Rabbi Eleazar both explain that as long as the Temple stood, the altar atoned for Israel, but now, one's table atones [when the poor are invited as guests]" (Talmud, tractate Berachoth 55a). Similarly, the liturgy of the Days of Awe (the High Holy Days; i.e. Rosh Hashanah and Yom Kippur) states that prayer, repentance and *tzedakah* atone for sin.

Judaism rejects the belief in "original sin." Both ancient and modern Judaism teaches that every person is responsible for his own actions. However, the existence of some "innate sinfulness on each human being was discussed" in both biblical (Genesis 8:21, Psalms 51.5) and post-biblical sources.

Some apocrypha and pseud epigraphic sources express pessimism about human nature ("A grain of evil seed was sown in Adam's heart from the beginning"), and the Talmud (b. Avodah Zarah 22b) has an unusual passage which Edward Kessler describes as "the serpent seduced Eve in paradise and impregnated her with spiritual-physical 'dirt' which was inherited through the generations," but the revelation at Sinai and the reception of the Torah cleansed Israel.[29] Kessler states that "although it is clear that belief in some form of original sin did exist in Judaism, it did not become mainstream teaching, nor dogmatically fixed," but remained at the margins of Judaism.

Moses and the Torah

Orthodox and Conservative Jews hold that the prophecy of Moses is held to be true; he is held to be the chief of all prophets, even of those who came before and after him. This belief was expressed by Maimonides, who wrote that "Moses was superior to all prophets, whether they preceded him or arose afterwards. Moses attained the highest possible human level. He perceived God to a degree surpassing every human that ever existed. God spoke to all other prophets through an intermediary. Moses alone did not need this; this is what the Torah means when God says "Mouth to mouth, I will speak to him." The great Jewish philosopher Philo understands this type of prophecy to be an extraordinarily high level of philosophical understanding, which had been reached by Moses and which enabled him to write the Torah through his own rational deduction of natural law. Maimonides, in his Commentary to the Mishna (preface to chapter "Chelek", Tractate Sanhedrin), and is his Mishneh Torah, (in the Laws of the foundations of the Torah, ch.7), describes a similar concept of prophecy, since a voice that did not originate from a body cannot exist, the understanding of Moses was based on his lofty philosophical understandings. However, this does not imply that the text of the Torah should be understood literally, as according to Karaism. Rabbinic tradition maintains that God conveyed not only the words of the Torah, but the meaning of the Torah. God gave rules as to how the laws were to be understood and implemented, and these were passed down as an oral tradition. This oral law was passed down from generation to generation and ultimately written down almost 2,000 years later in the Mishna and the two Talmuds.

For Reform Jews, the prophecy of Moses was not the highest degree of prophecy; rather it was the first in a long chain of progressive revelations in which mankind gradually began to understand the will of God better and better. As such, they maintain, that the laws of Moses are no longer binding, and it is today's generation that must assess what God wants of them. This principle is also rejected by most Reconstructionist Jews, but for a different reason; most posit that God is not a being with a will; thus they maintain that no will can be revealed.

The origin of the Torah

The Torah is composed of five books called in English Genesis, Exodus, Leviticus,

Numbers, and Deuteronomy. They chronicle the history of the Hebrews and also contain the commandments that Jews are to follow.

Rabbinic Judaism holds that the Torah extant today is the same one that was given to Moses by God on Mount Sinai. Maimonides explains: "We do not know exactly how the Torah was transmitted to Moses. But when it was transmitted, Moses merely wrote it down like a secretary taking dictation thus every verse in the Torah is equally holy, as they all originate from God, and are all part of God's Torah, which is perfect, holy and true."

Haredi Jews generally believe that the Torah today is no different from what was received from God to Moses, with only the most minor of scribal errors. Many other Orthodox Jews suggest that over the millennia, some scribal errors have crept into the Torah's text. They note that the Masoretes (7th to 10th centuries) compared all known Torah variations in order to create a definitive text. However, even according to this position that the scrolls that Jews possess today are not letter-perfect, the Torah scrolls are certainly the word-perfect textus receptus that was divinely revealed to Moses.

Indeed, the consensus of Orthodox rabbinic authority posits this belief in the word-perfect nature of the Torah scroll as representing a non-negotiable prerequisite for Orthodox Jewish membership.

Belief and the Belief in God's Law

Belief is the state of mind in which a person thinks something to be the case, with or without there being empirical evidence to prove that something is the case with factual certainty. In other words, belief is when someone thinks something is reality, true, when they have no absolute verified foundation for their certainty of the truth or realness of something. Another way of defining belief is, it is a mental representation of an attitude positively orientated towards the likelihood of something being true. In the context of Ancient Greek thought, two related concepts were identified with regards to the concept of belief: *pistis* and *doxa*. Simplified, we may say that pistis refers to *trust* and *confidence*, while doxa refers to *opinion* and *acceptance*. The English word *doctrine* is derived from *doxa*. Belief's purpose is to guide action and not to indicate truth.

In epistemology, philosophers use the term 'belief' to refer to personal attitudes associated with true or false ideas and concepts. However, 'belief' does not require active introspection and circumspection. For example, we never ponder whether or not the sun will rise. We simply assume the sun will rise. Since 'belief' is an important aspect of mundane life, according to the Stanford Encyclopedia of Philosophy, the question that must be answered is, "how a physical organism can have beliefs"

Religious belief refers to attitudes towards mythological, supernatural, or spiritual aspects of a religion. Religious belief is distinct from religious practice or religious behaviors with some believers not practicing religion and some practitioners not believing religion. Religious beliefs, being derived from ideas that are exclusive to religion, often relate to the existence, characteristics and worship of a deity or deities, divine intervention in the universe and human life, or the deontological explanations for the values and practices centered on the teachings of a spiritual leader or group.

In contrast to other belief systems, religious beliefs are usually codified.

Forms of religious belief

While it is popularly conceived that religions each have identifiable and exclusive sets of beliefs or creeds, surveys of religious belief have often found that the official doctrine and descriptions of the beliefs offered by religious authorities do not always agree with the privately held beliefs of those who identify as members of a particular religion.[32] A broad classification of the kinds of religious belief is documented below

Fundamentalism

First self-applied as a term to the conservative doctrine outlined by anti-modernist Protestants in the United States of America,[33] fundamentalism as a religious belief is associated with a strict adherence to an interpretation of scriptures that are generally associated with theologically conservative positions or traditional understandings of the text and are distrustful of innovative readings, new revelation, or alternate interpretations. Religious fundamentalism has been identified in the media as being associated with fanatical or zealous political movements around the world that have used a strict adherence to a particular religious doctrine as a means to establish political identity and enforce societal norms.

Orthodoxy

First used in the context of Early Christianity, orthodoxy is a religious belief that closely follows the edicts, apologies, and hermeneutics of a prevailing religious authority. In the case of Early Christianity, this authority was the communion of bishops, and is often referred to by the term [Magisterium]. The term *orthodox* was applied almost as an epithet to a group of Jewish believers who held to pre-Enlightenment understanding of Judaism and now known as Orthodox Judaism. The Eastern Orthodox Church of Christianity, as well as the Catholic Church, consider themselves to be the true heir to the Early Christian belief and practice. The antonym of orthodox is heterodox and those adhering to orthodoxy often accuse the heterodox of apostasy, schism, or heresy.

Modernism/reform

The Renaissance and later the Enlightenment in Europe were associated with varying degrees of religious tolerance and intolerance towards new religious ideas. The Philosophes took particular exception to many of the more fantastical claims of religions and directly challenged religious authority and the prevailing beliefs associated with the established churches. In response to the liberalizing political and social movements, some religious groups attempted to integrate Enlightenment ideals of rationality, equality, and individual liberty into their belief systems, especially into the nineteenth and twentieth centuries. Reform Judaism and Liberal Christianity are two examples of such religious associations.

Superstition

A term signifying derogation that is used by the religious and non-religious alike, superstition is the deprecated belief in supernatural causation. Those who deny the existence of the supernatural generally attribute all beliefs associated with it to be superstitious while a typical religious critique of superstition holds that it either encompasses beliefs in non-existent supernatural activity or that the supernatural activity is inappropriately feared or held in improper regard (see idolatry). Occultism, animism, paganism, and other folk religions were strongly condemned by Christian Churches as mean forms of superstition, though such condemnation did not necessarily eliminate the beliefs among the common people and many such religious beliefs persist to today.

Systemization

In Buddhism, practice and progress along the spiritual path happens when one follows the system of Buddhist practice. Any religion which follows (parts of) the fundamentals of this system has, according to the teachings of Buddha, good aspects to the extent it accords with this system. Any religion which goes against (parts of) the fundamentals of this system, includes bad aspects too. Any religion which does not teach certain parts of this system, is not because of this a 'bad' religion; it just lacks those teachings and is to that extent incomplete.

Universalism

Some believe that religion cannot be separated from other aspects of life, or believe that certain cultures did not or do not separate their religious activities from other activities in the same way that some people in modern Western cultures do.

Some would like to report cultures in which gods are involved in every aspect of life - if a cow goes dry, a god has caused this, and must be propitiated, when the sun rises in the morning, a god has caused this, and must be thanked. Even in modern Western cultures, many people see supernatural forces behind every event, as described by Carl Sagan in his book *The Demon-Haunted World*.

People with this worldview often consider the influence of Western culture to be inimical. Others with this world view resist the influence of science, and believe that science, or "so-called science", should be guided by religion. Still others with this worldview believe that all political decisions and laws should be guided by religion. This last belief is written into the constitution of many Islamic nations, and is shared by some fundamentalist Christians.

In addition, beliefs about
the supernatural or metaphysical may not presuppose a difference between any such thing as nature and non-nature, nor between science and what the most educated people believe.

Approaches to the beliefs of others

Adherents of particular religions deal with the differing doctrines and practices espoused by other religions in a variety of ways. All strains of thought appear in different segments of all major world religions.

Before God Created Humans

Although the Bible tells us very little about the period before God created humans, there are enough indicators available for us to draw some critical conclusions when it comes to the beginning of His laws. For it appears than in the very beginning, after God created His heavenly sons, He gave them no laws. He was simply their Father and He showed them the things that He wanted them to accomplish.

We draw this conclusion from the fact that until the Slanderer (Devil) rebelled and lied to Adam and Eve, there was no mention of a law to condemn him or other heavenly messengers to death. In fact, the first mention of a penalty for his disobedience is found at Genesis 3:15, where the curse on the snake (and the one behind its words) was cryptically foretold to be a 'watching for its head.'

So if there were no laws from God (and we can't dogmatically say that there weren't), why hadn't He created them? For He obviously realized that His sons could choose to rebel, because He deliberately created each of them with the ability to do whatever they wished to do. And for the heavenly sons, both right and wrong and the results of displeasing God must have been obvious. Therefore, it appears as though God didn't want to start off their relationship with Him on a negative footing by even discussing what would happen should they choose to disobey Him.

But, what incentive would there be for that spirit person who made himself the Slanderer (gr. *Diabolos* or *Devil*) to openly defy God? Well, as the results proved (Revelation

12:4 tells us that, 'a third of the stars of heaven' were dragged to the earth), his motivation was a desire for power, and he knew that he had raised an issue that all living creatures both in heaven and on the earth would be watching.

The First Law

The first law that we read of in the Bible is the simple one that was given to Adam in the Paradise of Delights, when God told him not to eat from the fruit of the tree of knowledge of good and bad. And a penalty was also spelled out, should they choose to disobey: death to the offender.

Think of what the creation of this simple rule must have meant for all of God's heavenly sons. For it showed for the first time what God's sentence would be for those who willingly chose to rebel against Him... returning no nonexistence. And for this one who had likely already made himself the first universal rebel; he had a stake in seeing this rule broken. So he set out to challenge God by lying to the first humans and leading them to disobey the law, which would then raise the question before all living creatures everywhere, of whether God has the right to expect their obedience and love.

It's interesting that God's law to Adam and Eve was so simple. Once again, no negative thoughts of the possibility of murder, theft, rape, or any of the hundreds of other human vices were mentioned. There was just the one command: 'This is mine, so don't touch it!'

The First Murder

When we think of the worst crime that is possible for us to commit, we usually think of murder. And as might be expected, the second sin mentioned in the Bible was when Cain murdered his brother, Abel. And here, it is interesting to note that God's penalty on Cain wasn't death, but the curse of having to live a hard life.

Recognize that apparently there was no law up until then that forbade murder. There was just the good example set by God's love, and what we call 'conscience' or good sense, to tell all intelligent living creatures what was right and wrong. Yet, as the Bible tells us, murder and other human vices continued to increase to the point that, as it says, 'God saw all the badness that men were doing on the earth was increasing and that the entire motivation of their hearts was always twisted toward evil.'

So, except for the righteous man Noah and his family; He destroyed all of humanity and much of the animal kingdom.

God's Laws After the Downpour

After Noah and his family left the ark, God gave him some basic guidelines as to what would happen to those who did extremely bad things. You can't really call them laws, because He didn't tell men what not to do, He simply told them what results to expect if they were guilty of wrong conduct. These rules are often thought of being part of what is called, 'the Rainbow Covenant.' Here's what God said at Genesis 9:3-6: 'All living and slithering animals can serve as meat for you… I have given them all to you as though they were green vegetation.

But you must not eat flesh with its blood of life. Otherwise, I will require your blood at the hand of all the wild animals. I will also require a man's life at the hand of his human brothers.

Whoever spills the blood of men will also have their blood spilled, because I made man in the image of God.'

So there were just two evil actions that He said would

provide bad results. They were:

1. The blood of animals was not to be eaten (it was to be poured out as some sort of a sacrifice to God); otherwise, the violator was liable to be killed by wild animals

2. Any man who murdered another was liable to be killed by fellow humans.

Recognize that since these instructions were given to the common forefather of all of us, they still apply to us, no matter what traditions, modern ideas, or so-called 'politically-correct' thinking may teach us. And while the ban on murder is quite well understood, the reason for the warning against eating animal blood is particularly interesting. Remember that in God's instructions to Adam in the Paradise and also to Noah following the downpour (flood), men were told to 'rule over the fish of the seas, the winged creatures of the skies, all the herding animals of the ground, all the slithering animals that crawl on the ground, and the whole earth.' So, notice that He didn't say anything in the beginning about us being allowed to kill and eat the animals that were entrusted to our care. However, likely due to what had become common practice prior to the downpour, God told Noah that men could eat the animals, as long as they poured the blood, which He described in Hebrew as the *ruach* or in Greek as the *psyche* (*soul* or *life*) on the ground. So, what conclusions may we reach from all the above? The evidence shows that the making of laws and rules wasn't God's way. Rather, these things were forced on Him by the inventiveness and badness of humans and of the rebellious desires of the spirit sons of God.

The Law to Moses

However, because men really didn't understand all of God's righteous ways, He did provide an extensive list of laws to govern His nation (Israel), after He delivered them from bondage in Egypt. And the foundations for these laws (all of which are related in detail from Exodus through Deuteronomy) are what we call the Ten Commandments. What did the Old Law accomplish? Well, Paul explained it when he wrote (at Romans 3:19, 20): 'We know that everything which was said in the Law was meant for just those who are under the Law… yet it stopped every mouth and made the whole world deserving of God's punishment. **But now, no flesh is going to be called righteous before Him by obedience to the Law, because the Law just helped us to understand what sin is**.'

Then he wrote (at Romans 3:27, 28): 'So, where is our reason for boasting? It's gone! Does it come from our obedience to the Law? No, it comes through the Law of Faith, **since we believe that a man is called righteous because of his faith, not by the works of the Law!**'

And at Romans 5:20, 21, we read: 'Now, the Law came along so as to show up many errors. However, where there are many sins, a superabundance of loving-care can be shown. **Therefore, as sin has reigned and brought death; God's loving care will bring a righteous rule and age-long life through our Lord Jesus, the Anointed**.'

Yet, despite all that Paul wrote, many religious people today still think that they will be declared righteous by following the Old Law, which they wrongly believe was given to all of mankind, not just to Israel. But as Paul pointed out in his numerous letters; though the principles of God's thinking are all there as a guide to living a righteous life, this Law was impossible for imperfect humans to keep. And so, one of the reasons why Jesus gave his life for us was to do away with that old Sacred Agreement of Laws and to make a New Sacred agreement with us, the laws of which are simply to love God and to love each other. For righteous people don't really need laws to tell them right from wrong.

As Paul wrote (at Romans 13:10): 'Love doesn't do bad things to one's neighbor, **for the Law is fulfilled through love.**.' He also wrote (at Romans 3:28): **'We believe that a man is called righteous because of his faith, not by the works of the Law!'**

Were the Old Laws Harsh?

Whenever people wish to degrade the Bible, they point to the old laws and their penalties, claiming them to be the product of a harsh and unloving God. Yet, if you understand the purpose of these laws, you'll see that they weren't really harsh or oppressive, because nobody was really required to follow them other than those who freely choose to live in the land of Israel!

It was God's land and He gave it to the people who wanted to be parties to His Sacred Agreement. And all who wished to live in this sacred land (Israelites and gentiles alike), since they claimed to be His people, were required to follow the rules and laws that He set down for them. Then, to show that they were part of this sacred relationship, He said that all males had to have the sign of circumcision on their flesh, and He told them how to dress, how to groom themselves, and how to act.

Realize that the land had been set aside not just for Israel, but for all who wished to serve God. And any who didn't want to be part of this relationship were free to go wherever they wished and to dress and act however they wished… the story of the prodigal son well illustrates this.

So, why were such apparently minor infractions as breaking the Sabbath or entering God's Temple in an unclean condition punishable by death? Not because God considered such things major sins, but because anyone who deliberately chose to disobey Him and yet live in His sacred land had to be dealt with in a deliberate way to maintain the cleanliness and sacred purpose of that land.

The Period of the Judges

Probably no period in time better illustrates God's purposes and ways than the period of the judges in Israel. For, although the people had God's Law, there was no government as we know it, or civil administration in the land. All they had was judges who were appointed by God to decide legal matters and to take the lead in war, when necessary. There were no politicians to make laws and no policemen to enforce them; the people were just trusted to know right from wrong. Why, it was the Israelites who demanded human kings, along with all their taxes, legislators, local laws, and the foibles of human rule.

Laws and Rules Aren't God's Way

As we can see from all the above; although God was responsible for the first law (not to eat of the tree of knowledge of good and bad), the making of laws isn't His way. In fact, that's why Jesus so strongly condemned the Pharisees; because, in their quest for self-righteousness, they looked at the principles of what God considered to be good and bad, and turned these principles into laws for 'righteous' people to follow. Yet, 'Christian' religions continue to follow this same practice today by setting out lists of rules that they have created, but which aren't specifically outlined in the Bible.

However, as any person's good sense and conscience would

tell them; there are in fact things that people who love God just shouldn't do.

Paul outlined them at 1 Corinthians 6:9,10:

'Don't make any mistake about this; Sexually immoral people, idol worshipers, adulterers, gays, men who have sex with men, thieves, greedy people, drunkards, insulters, and extortionists, won't inherit God's Kingdom.'

Realize that Paul wasn't laying out Christian 'Laws' here. He was simply enumerating things that a good conscience should tell us aren't right.

There are also some things that God warned against practicing back in Genesis and which love of God would forbid us from doing. These were repeated by Peter, James, and John when laying out the guidelines for Gentile converts to Christianity at Acts 21:25: 'As for the gentile believers; we've already sent them our decision to stay free from things that are sacrificed to idols, from blood, from what is strangled, and from sexual immorality.'

Note that this mention of blood and strangulation (where the blood isn't poured out) reminds us that God's instructions to Noah were still viewed as important by early Christians… as were the other instructions against immorality and worship of idols.

Principles

Principles are the basis for God's laws… they are the reasons behind His laws. And if you were to read the entire Law of Moses, you would have a much better understanding of God thoughts on many matters. They are the guidelines we can refer to in order to make wise decisions.

However, it has often been said that principles are more

important than laws, because God's laws for mankind have changed, depending on the circumstances, while His principles remain the same. And though this is true, we must understand that God's laws have always been far more important than obedience to the principles. Whereas principles are general guidelines, His laws are the dividing lines, and He has used His inspired servants to write them down in the Bible so we would know the difference. Remember that laws are greater, because they are also principles, but principles that God felt strongly enough about to turn into laws.

When Men Turn Principles into Laws

Now, in the past, whenever someone felt that he or she could take Bible principles and turn them into laws for others to follow; the Bible plainly shows that God considers this a serious sin. The Pharisees, for example, were guilty of turning principles into laws, and Jesus condemned them for doing it. As you read the Gospels, notice the many ways they did this in regard to matters of tithing, washing, the Sabbath, the way they dressed, etc.

What's wrong with turning principles into laws? Well, as is so typical of man-made laws; back when they were under the Law of Moses, the Pharisees made up rules that went well beyond the Law. Yet, despite the fact that Jesus recognized the righteous principles behind their rules, he still condemned them as hypocrites. He didn't say, 'Well, they had good motives' (as some have done today), because they didn't; and it was their self-righteous creation of religious rules that condemned them... as it condemns all who think they can add to God's laws.

Yet, through the years, super-righteous religious leaders have continued to follow the lead of the Pharisees in creating their own laws of right and wrong, based on Bible principles (which is obviously displeasing to God). We see such rules being made today in regard to recreation, the way we dress, the things we eat and drink, in matters of bathing and washing, unhealthy habits (such as smoking), in private relations between husbands and wives, and in innumerable other matters. And yes; while good sense and manners should be everyone's desire and suggestions may be given, making religious rules about such things goes 'beyond the things that are written' (1 Corinthians 4:6). Understand that virtually all religious laws are the laws of men, not God. As Paul explained it at Romans 6:14: **'So, sin must not be your master; because, you aren't under Law, you're under God's loving care.'**

Recognize that God's principles are all laid out in the Old Law. And if we turn these principles back into laws again, we are putting ourselves back under the Old Sacred Agreement, which Paul showed time and again to be something that is unnecessary and wrong, since we are all under the New Sacred Agreement, which is based on love, not laws! And if there are those who still wish to argue that they have the right to set out Bible principles as laws; consider the fact that God spoke of eating creatures that live in the water which don't have fins or scales (such as catfish, shrimp, oysters, lobster, scallops, crabs, etc.) as something **disgusting** (at Leviticus 11:9-12).

And please don't (as some readers have done) turn that into a law!

The point is; there are many Bible principles that people commonly consider to be less important. And since, under the Rainbow Covenant, God allowed mankind to eat all sorts of animals; we have to assume that the dietary laws of Israel were just for them. So, recognize that Christians aren't bound by the Old Law or even its principles that the unrighteous wish to turn into modern rules. Notice how Jesus himself showed that rules about things we eat (for example) should not be our concern. For he said (as recorded at Matthew 15:16, 17):'

Don't you get the point? Don't you realize that whatever you put into your mouth goes into your belly and then into the sewer?
But the things that come out of the mouth come from the heart... these are the things that dirty a man!'

Are God's Laws the Final Word?

So, is it true that God's laws are the final word on the matter? No, for many stories in the Bible show us how righteousness and good sense outweigh even God's rules and laws. Take for example, God's instructions to the Israelites to destroy all the people in the Promised Land. Yet, when the spies entered Jericho, they vowed to spare the lives of a prostitute named RaHab and her entire family because of her trust in God's power.

Then later on, the Israelites unwitting made a peace agreement with the people of the city of Gibeon, because they were fooled into doing it. Yet the Israelites honored that agreement and let those people live, because they had sworn to do so... and this breaking of His Law was blessed by God.

As you can see, Laws never come before righteousness. Rather, righteousness is the purpose and basis of God's laws.

So His instructions could be summed up as, 'Don't do anything that is overtly bad. Use your Christian-trained consciences, and when in doubt, do whatever shows that you love God and your fellow humans, and that you even respect the value of the lives of the animals that you were created to rule over.'

Finding God's Forgiveness

The Bible tells us that there is no man who doesn't sin (see 1 Kings 8:46). Therefore, it is important for us to talk to Him about such things regularly, so He doesn't come to view us as unrepentant sinners (see Romans 2:5-7). We should never try to justify or cover over the bad things that we've done before Him, because this indicates a bad heart and bad motives... and admitting our sins to God is a very difficult thing to do!

God also requires that we turn from our bad ways. And if we do, even the worst things that we've done can be can be forgiven. For we are told at Isaiah 1:16-18:

The 13 Principles of Faith

Rabbi Moses ben Maimon, better known as Maimonides or "The Rambam" (1135–1204 CE), lived at a time when both Christianity and Islam were developing active theologies. Jewish scholars were often asked to attest to their faith by their counterparts in other religions. The Rambam's 13 principles of faith were formulated in his commentary on the Mishnah (tractate Sanhedrin, chapter 10). They were one of several efforts by Jewish theologians in the Middle Ages to create such a list. By the time of Maimonides, centers of Jewish learning and law were dispersed geographically. Judaism no longer had a central authority that might bestow official approval on his principles of faith.

Maimonides' 13 principles were controversial when first proposed, evoking criticism by Crescas and Joseph Albo. They evoked criticism as minimizing acceptance of the entire Torah (Rabbi S. of Montpelier, Yad Rama, Y. Alfacher, Rosh Amanah). The 13 principles were ignored by much of the Jewish community for the next few centuries. (*Dogma in Medieval Jewish Thought*, Menachem Kellner). Over time two poetic restatements of these principles (*Ani Ma'amin* and *Yigdal*) became canonized in the Jewish. Eventually, Maimonides' 13 principles of faith became the mostly widely accepted statement of belief.

Importantly, Maimonides, while enumerating the above, added the following caveat "There is no difference between [the Biblical statement] 'his wife was Mehithabel' [Genesis 10,6] on the one hand [i.e. an "unimportant" verse], and 'Hear, O Israel' on the other [i.e. an "important" verse]... anyone who denies even such verses thereby denies God and shows contempt for his teachings more than any other skeptic, because he holds that the Torah can be divided into essential and non-essential parts..." The uniqueness of the 13 fundamental beliefs was that even a rejection out of ignorance placed one outside Judaism, whereas the rejection of the rest of Torah must be a conscious act to stamp one as an unbeliever. Others, such as Rabbi Joseph Albo and the Raavad, criticized Maimonides' list as containing items that, while true, in their opinion did not place those who rejected them out of ignorance in the category of heretic. Many others criticized any such formulation as minimizing acceptance of the entire Torah (see above). As noted, however, neither Maimonides nor his contemporaries viewed these principles as encompassing all of Jewish belief, but rather as the core theological underpinnings of the acceptance of Judaism.

Several Orthodox scholars write that the popular Orthodox understanding of these principles are not at all what Maimonides held to be true. See books noted below by

Marc Shapiro and Menachem Kellner.

After Maimonides

The successors of Maimonides, from the 13th to the 15th century — Nahmanides, Abba Mari ben Moses, Simon ben Zemah Duran, Joseph Albo, Isaac Arama, and Joseph Jaabez — narrowed his 13 articles to three core beliefs: Belief in God; in Creation (or revelation); and in providence (or retribution).

Others, like Crescas and David ben Samuel Estella, spoke of seven fundamental articles, laying stress on free-will. On the other hand, David ben Yom-Tob ibn Bilia, in his "Yesodot ha- Maskil" (Fundamentals of the Thinking Man), adds to the 13 of Maimonides 13 of his own — a number which a contemporary of Albo also chose for his fundamentals; while Jedaiah Penini, in the last chapter of his "Behinat ha-Dat," enumerated no less than 35 cardinal principles.

Isaac Abravanel, his "Rosh Amanah," took the same attitude towards Maimonides' creed. While defending Maimonides against Hasdai and Albo, he refused to accept dogmatic articles for Judaism, criticizing any formulation as minimizing acceptance of all 613 mitzvot.

Faith itself is not a religious concept in Judaism. The only one-time *faith in God* is mentioned in the 24 books of the Jewish Bible, is in verse 10 of the Book of Isaiah, Chapter 43. In this verse, the commandment to know God is followed by the commandments to believe and to understand, thus denoting descending importance.

However, Judaism does recognize the positive value of *Emunah*[35] (generally translated as faith, trust in God)

and the negative status of the *Apikorus* (heretic), but faith is not as stressed or as central as it is in other religions, especially compared with Christianity and Islam. It could be a necessary means for being a practicing religious Jew, but the emphasis is placed on true knowledge,
true prophecy and practice rather than on faith itself. Very rarely does it relate to any teaching that must be believed. Judaism does not require one to explicitly identify God (a key tenet of Christian faith, which is called Avodah Zarah in Judaism, a minor form of idol worship, a big sin and strictly forbidden to Jews). Rather, in Judaism, one is to honor a (personal) idea of God, supported by the many principles quoted in the Talmud to define Judaism, mostly by what it is not. Thus there is no established formulation of Jewish principles of faith which are mandatory for all (observant) Jews.

In the Jewish scriptures trust in God - *Emunah* - refers to how God acts toward his people and how they are to respond to him; it is rooted in the everlasting covenant established in the Torah, notably[36] Deuteronomy 7:9:

Know, therefore, that the Lord, your God He is God, the faithful God, who keeps the covenant and loving kindness with those who love Him and keep His commandments to a thousand generations.

Tanach, Devarim 7:9

The specific tenets that compose required belief and their application to the times have been disputed throughout Jewish history. Today many, but not all, Orthodox Jews have accepted Maimonides' Thirteen Principles of Belief.[38][39]

A traditional example of *Emunah* as seen in the Jewish annals is found in the person of Abraham. On a number of occasions, Abraham both accepts statements from God that seem impossible and offers obedient actions in response to direction from God to do things that seem implausible (Genesis 12-15).

"The Talmud describes how a thief also believes in God: On the brink of his forced entry, as he is about to risk his life—and the life of his victim—he cries out with all sincerity, 'God help me!' The thief has faith that there is a God who hears his cries, yet it escapes him that this God may be able to provide for him without requiring that he abrogate God's will by stealing from others. For *emunah* to affect him in this way he needs study and contemplation."

The 13 Principles of faith are as follows:

1. Belief in the existence of the Creator, who is perfect in every manner of existence and is the Primary Cause of all that exists.

2. The belief in God's absolute and unparalleled unity.

3. The belief in God's non-corporeality, nor that He will be affected by any physical occurrences, such as movement, or rest, or dwelling.

4. The belief in God's eternity.

5. The imperative to worship God exclusively and no foreign false gods.

6. The belief that God communicates with man through prophecy.

7. The belief in the primacy of the prophecy of Moses our teacher.

8. The belief in the divine origin of the Torah.

9. The belief in the immutability of the Torah.

10. The belief in God's omniscience and providence.

11. The belief in divine reward and retribution.

12. The belief in the arrival of the Messiah and the messianic era.

13. The belief in the resurrection of the dead.

The word translated as "faith" in the New Testament is the Greek word πίστις which can also be translated "belief" or "trust". There are various views in Christianity regarding the nature of faith. Some see faith as being persuaded or convinced that something is true.[11] In this view, a person believes something when they are presented with adequate evidence that it is true. Theologian Greg Boyd argues to the contrary, that faith includes doubt.

Then there are numerous views regarding the results of faith. Some believe that true faith results in good works, while others believe that while faith in Jesus brings eternal life, it does not necessarily result in good works.

Regardless of which approach to faith a Christian takes, all agree that the Christian faith is aligned with the ideals and the example of the life of Jesus. The Christian sees the mystery of God and his grace and seeks to know and become obedient to God. To a Christian, faith is not static but causes one to learn more of God and to grow; Christian faith has its origin in God.

In Christianity, faith causes change as it seeks a greater understanding of God. Faith is not fideism or simple obedience to a set of rules or statements. Before Christians have faith, they must understand in whom and in what they have faith. Without understanding, there cannot be true faith, and that understanding is built on the foundation of the community of believers, the scriptures and traditions and on the personal experiences of the believer. In English translations of the New Testament, the word "faith" generally corresponds to the Greek noun πίστις (*pistis*) or to the Greek verb πιστεύω (*pisteuo*), meaning "to trust, to have confidence, faithfulness, to be reliable, to assure".

In Islam, a believer's faith in the metaphysical aspects of Islam is called "Iman" (Arabic: الإيمان), which is complete submission to the will of God, not unquestionable or blind belief. A man must build his faith on well-grounded convictions beyond any reasonable doubt and above uncertainty. According to the Quran, Iman must be accompanied by righteous deeds and the two together are necessary for entry into Paradise. In the Hadith of Gabriel, *Iman* in addition to *Islam* and *Ihsan* form the three dimensions of the Islamic religion.

Prophet Muhammad referred to the six articles of faith in the Hadith of Gabriel: "Iman is that you believe in God and His Angels and His Books and His Messengers and the Hereafter and the good and evil fate [ordained by your God]." The first five are mentioned together in the Qur'an The Quran states that faith can grow with remembrance of God. The Qur'an also states that nothing in this world should be dearer to a true believer than faith.

Enlightenment

Enlightenment refers to the "full comprehension of a situation". It is commonly used to denote the Age of Enlightenment, but is also used in Western cultures in a religious context. It translates several Buddhist terms and concepts, most notably *bodhi*, *kensho* and *satori*. Related terms from Asian religions are *moksha* (liberation) in Hinduism, *Kevala Jnana* in Jainism and *ushta* in Zoroastrianism.

In Christianity, the word "enlightenment" is rarely used, except to refer to the Age of Enlightenment and its influence on Christianity.

Roughly equivalent terms in Christianity maybe illumination, kenosis, metanoia, revelation, salvation and conversion.

The word "enlightenment" is not generally used in Christian contexts for religious understanding or insight. More commonly used terms in the Christian tradition are religious conversion and revelation.

An Islamic Perspective of Enlightenment It is important that we first understand enlightenment and its Islamic nature. The Quran describes the human being as the best of creations, and this claim is premised on the human ability to reason (95:4). We have indeed created man in the best of molds (Quran 95:4) The Quran does not invite blind followers; it demands and exhorts us to reflect and use our reason to read God's signs in nature, history, and text (12:109). In all its presentations, the Quran presents evidence and proofs and, indeed, demands arguments and proofs from those who disbelieve its message. There is no suggestion or expectation in the Quran that the human being ceases to be the best of creations and becomes an ape (reversing evolution!). The Quran does not ask believers to surrender their reasoning capacity, the very faculty on which it is relying for the cognition of God. It is reason, not ritual, which connects humanity with the divine, and this theme is the central essence of the Quran. Until the guardians of Islam and Muslims, their intellectuals, and their Ulema realize and emphasize this at every opportunity, the Muslim community will remain immature.

Furqan means "criterion for judgment" or "capacity to discern." It also means to differentiate between the right and wrong, and between justice and injustice. This understanding of the Quran implies that the Prophet's personality, which is the prototype What is Enlightenment? Journal of Religion & Society 5 16 (2014) for a Muslim, is the embodiment of the capacity to judge. If this is what Ayesha meant, then it means that to be like the Prophet is to have Furqan, which is to be capable of discernment. One of the enduring myths of Islamic beliefs is the extreme glorification of early Muslims. Muslim scholars, searching for authority (necessary in the absence of reason) to support their interpretations of Islam created a hierarchy of interpretive privilege in Islam. The veracity of a particular opinion depends upon the personality and reputation of the person with whom it corresponds. The Prophet is on the top of the pyramid, followed by his companions, then come the companions of the companions, followed by the classical scholars. While the status of the Prophet is indubitable, the rest of the pyramid weighs upon the reason of subsequent generations of Muslims to the point that today, even to disagree with a companion or with one of the classical scholars leads to calls for excommunication (takfir) and even endangers life itself. Islamic scholars have subtly propagated the myth that early Muslims are far superior in intellect and virtue than later Muslims no matter what the issue is and, therefore, contemporary understandings and interpretations must defer to past understandings and interpretations.

Reward and punishment

The mainstream Jewish view is that God will reward those who observe His commandments and punish those who intentionally transgress them. Examples of rewards and punishments are described throughout the Bible, and throughout classical rabbinic literature: see Free will in Jewish thought. The common understanding of this principle is accepted by most Orthodox and Conservative and many Reform Jews; it is generally rejected by the Reconstructionist.

The Bible contains references to Sheol, lit. *gloom*, as the common destination of the dead, which may be compared with the Hades or underworld of ancient religions. In later tradition this is interpreted either as Hell or as a literary expression for death or the grave in general.

According to aggadic passages in the Talmud, God judges who has followed His commandments and who does not and to what extent. Those who do not "pass the test" go to a purifying place (sometimes referred to as *Gehinnom*, i.e. Hell, but more analogous to the Christian Purgatory) to "learn their lesson". There is, however, for the most part, no eternal damnation. The vast majority of souls only go to that reforming place for a limited amount of time (less than one year).

Certain categories are spoken of as having "no part in the world to come", but this appears to mean annihilation rather than an eternity of torment.

Philosophical rationalists such as Maimonides believed that God did not actually mete out rewards and punishments as such. In this view, these were beliefs that were necessary for the masses to believe in order to maintain a structured society and to encourage the observance of Judaism.

However, once one learned Torah properly, one could then learn the higher truths. In this view, the nature of the reward is that if a person perfected his intellect to the highest degree, then the part of his intellect that connected to God – the active intellect – would be immortalized and enjoy the "Glory of the Presence" for all eternity. The punishment would simply be that this would not happen; no part of one's intellect would be immortalized with God. See Divine Providence in Jewish thought.

The Kabbalah (mystical tradition in Judaism) contains further elaborations, though some Jews do not consider these authoritative. For example, it admits the possibility of reincarnation, which is generally rejected by non-mystical Jewish theologians and philosophers. It also believes in a triple soul, of which the lowest level (*nefesh* or animal life) dissolves into the elements, the middle layer (*ruach* or intellect) goes to *Gan Eden* (Paradise) while the highest level (*neshamah* or spirit) seeks union with God.

Many Jews consider "Tikkun Olam" (or Repairing the world) as a fundamental motivating factor in Jewish ethics. Therefore, the concept of "life after death," in the Jewish view, is not encouraged as the motivating factor in performance of Judaism. Indeed, it is held that one can attain closeness to God even in this world through moral and spiritual perfection.

Israel chosen for a purpose

God chose the Jewish people to be in a unique covenant with God; the description of this covenant is the Torah itself. Contrary to popular belief, Jewish people do not simply say that "God chose the Jews." This claim, by itself, exists nowhere in the Tanakh (the Jewish Bible). Such a claim could imply that God loves only the Jewish people, that only Jews can be close to God, and that only Jews can have a heavenly reward. The actual claim made is that the Jews were chosen for a specific mission, a duty: to be a light unto the nations, and to have a covenant with God as described in the Torah.

Reconstructionist Judaism rejects even this variant of choosiness as morally defunct.

Rabbi Lord Immanuel Jakobovits, former Chief Rabbi of the United Synagogue of Great Britain, describes the mainstream Jewish view on this issue: "Yes, I do believe that the chosen people concept as affirmed by Judaism in its holy writ, its prayers, and its millennial tradition. In fact, I believe that every people—and indeed, in a more limited way, every individual—is 'chosen' or destined for some distinct purpose in advancing the designs of Providence. Only, some fulfill their mission and others do not. Maybe the Greeks were chosen for their unique contributions to art and philosophy, the Romans for their pioneering services in law and government, the British for bringing parliamentary rule into the world, and the Americans for piloting democracy in a pluralistic society. The Jews were chosen by God to be 'peculiar unto Me' as the pioneers of religion and morality; that was and is their national purpose."

References:

Emunah

Louis Jacobs, "Chapter 2: The Unity of God" in *A Jewish Theology* (1973). Behrman House.

Deut 6:4–9

Aryeh Kaplan, *The Handbook of Jewish Thought* (1979). e Maznaim: p. 9.

Jewish Theology and Process Thought (eds. Sandra B. Lubarsky & David Ray Griffin). SUNY Press, 1996.

How Old is the Universe? How Old is the Universe?, NASA; Phil Plait, The Universe Is 13.82 Billion Years Old (March 21, 2013), *Slate*

Norbert Max Samuelson, *Revelation and the God of Israel* (2002). Cambridge University Press: p. 126.

Angel, Marc (1995). Leon Klenicki and Geoffrey Wigoder, ed. A Dictionary of the Jewish-Christian Dialogue (Expanded ed.). Paulist Press. p. 40. ISBN 0809135825.

Maimonides, *The Guide of the Perplexed*, translated by Chaim Menachem Rabin(Hackett, 1995).

Dan Cohn-Sherbok, *Judaism: History, Belief, and Practice* (2003). Psychology Press: p. 359.

Louis Jacobs, "Chapter 6: Eternity" in *A Jewish Theology* (1973). Behrman House: p. 81-93.

Clark M. Williamson, *A Guest in the House of Israel: Post-Holocaust Church Theology* (1993). Westminster John Knox Press: pp. 210-215.

Louis Jacobs, "Chapter 5: Omnipotence and Omniscience" in *A Jewish Theology* (1973). Behrman House: p. 76-77.

Samuel S. Cohon. *What We Jews Believe* (1931). Union of American Hebrew Congregations.

Edward Kessler, *What Do Jews Believe? The Customs and Culture of Modern Judaism* (2007). Bloomsbury Publishing: pp. 42-44.

Morris N. Kertzer, *What Is a Jew* (1996). Simon and Schuster: pp. 15-16.

Joseph Telushkin, *Jewish Literacy: The Most Important Things to Know About the Jewish Religion, Its People, and Its History* (Revised Edition) (2008). HarperCollins: p. 472.

http://www.pewforum.org/files/2013/05/report-religious-landscape-study-full.pdf, p. 164

Ronald H. Isaacs, Every Person's Guide to Jewish Philosophy and Philosophers (1999). Jason Aronson: pp 50-51.

Meir Bar-Illan, "Prayers of Jews to Angels and Other Mediators in the First Centuries CE" in *Saints and Role Models in Judaism and Christianity* (eds. Joshua Schwartz and Marcel Poorthuis), pp. 79-95.

Peter A. Pettit, "Hebrew Bible" in *A Dictionary of Jewish-Christian Relations* (2005). Eds. Edward Kessler and Neil Wenborn. Cambridge University Press.

Christopher Hugh Partridge, *Introduction to World Religions* (2005). Fortress Press: pp 283-286.

Jacob Neusner, *The Talmud: What It Is and What It Says* (2006). Rowman & Littlefield.

Adin Steinsaltz, "Chapter 1: What is the Talmud?" in *The Essential Talmud* (2006). Basic Books: pp. 3-9.

Determinism, in *The Oxford Dictionary of the Jewish Religion* (ed. Adele Berlin, Oxford University Press, 2011), p. 210.

Louis Jacobs, *A Jewish Theology* (Behrman House, 1973), p. 79.

Alan Brill, *Thinking God: The Mysticism of Rabbi Zadok of Lublin* (KTAV Publishing, 2002), p. 134.

Ronald L. Eisenberg, *What the Rabbis Said: 250 Topics from the Talmud* (2010). ABC-CLIO: pp. 311-313.

Edward Kessler, "Original Sin" in *A Dictionary of Jewish-Christian Relations*(eds. Edward Kessler & Neil Wenborn, Cambridge University Press, 2005) pp. 323-324.

Rebecca Alpert (2011). "Judaism, Reconstructionist". The Cambridge Dictionary of Judaism and Jewish Culture. Cambridge University Press. p. 346

Marc Angel, "Afterlife" in *A Dictionary of the Jewish-Christian Dialogue* (1995). Eds. Leon Klenicki and Geoffrey Wigoder. Paulist Press: pp. 3-5.

Jump up to:[a b c] Eugene B. Borowitz, Naomi Patz, "Chapter 19: Our Hope for a Messianic Age" in *Explaining Reform Judaism* (1985). Behrman House.

David Birnbaum, Jews, Church & Civilization, Volume III (Millennium Education Foundation 2005)

"Declaration of Principles – "The Pittsburgh Platform"". The Central Conference of American Rabbis. 1885. Retrieved 2012-05-21.

"The Guiding Principles of Reform Judaism – "The Columbus Platform"". The Central Conference of American Rabbis. 1937. Retrieved 2012-05-21.

"Reform Judaism: A Centenary Perspective". The Central Conference of American Rabbis. 1976. Retrieved 2012-05-21.

"A Statement of Principles for Reform Judaism". The Central Conference of American Rabbis. 1999. Retrieved 2012-05-21.

Mordecai M. Kaplan, Judaism as a Civilization: Toward a Reconstruction of American-Jewish Life (MacMillan Company 1934), reprinted by Jewish Publication Society 2010.

Eric Caplan, From Ideology to Liturgy: Reconstructionist Worship and American Liberal Judaism (Hebrew Union College Press 2002)

"Pillars of Islam". Encyclopedia Online. Retrieved 2007-05-02.

"Pillars of Islam". Oxford Centre for Islamic Studies. United Kingdom: Oxford University. Retrieved 2010-11-17.

"Five Pillars". United Kingdom: Public Broadcasting Service (PBS). Retrieved 2010-11-17.

"The Five Pillars of Islam". Canada: University of Calgary. Retrieved 2010-11-17.

"The Five Pillars of Islam". United Kingdom: BBC. Retrieved 2010-11-17.

Pillars of Islam , Oxford Islamic Studies Online

Hooker, Richard (July 14, 1999). "arkan ad-din the five pillars of religion". United States: Washington State University. Archived from the original on 2010-12-03. Retrieved 2010-11-17.

"Religions". The World Factbook. United States: Central Intelligence Agency. 2010. Retrieved 2010-08-25.

Hajj

From the article on the Pillars of Islam in Oxford Islamic Studies Online

Matthew S. Gordon and Martin Palmer, "Islam", Info base Publishing, 2009. Books.Google.fr. p. 87. Retrieved 2012-08-26.

Ridgeon (2003), p.258

Zakat, *Encyclopedia of Islam Online*

Zakat Alms-giving

Quran 2:183–187

Quran 2:196

Quran 33:35

Fasting, *Encyclopedia of the Qur'an* (2005)

Farah (1994), p.144-145

talhaanjum_9

Esposito (1998), p.90,91

Tabatabaei (2002), p. 211,213

"For whom fasting is mandatory". USC-MSA Compendium of Muslim Texts. Archived from the original on 8 March 2007. Retrieved 2007-04-18.

Quran 2:184

Khan (2006), p. 54

Islam, *The New Encyclopedia Britannica* (2005)

Farah (1994), p.145-147

Hoiberg (2000), p.237–238

Goldschmidt (2005), p.48

See chapter on "Islamic Beliefs (the Pillars of Islam)" in Invitation to Islam by Sayed Moustafa Al-Qazwini. http://www.al-islam.org/invitation/

Walsh, John Evangelist. *Walking shadows: Orson Welles, William Randolph Hearst, and Citizen Kane.* Madison, Wisconsin: University of Wisconsin Press/Popular Press, 2004.

"Isma'ilism". Retrieved 2007-04-24.

Swinburne, R.G. "God" in Honderich, Ted. (ed)*The Oxford Companion to Philosophy*, Oxford University Press, 1995.

Platinga, Alvin. "God, Arguments for the Existence of", *Routledge Encyclopedia of Philosophy*, Routledge, 2000.

Jan Assmann, *Religion and Cultural Memory: Ten Studies*, Stanford University Press 2005, p.59

M. Lichtheim, *Ancient Egyptian Literature*, Vol.2, 1980, p.96

Freud, S. (1939). Moses and Monotheism: Three Essays.

Gunther Siegmund Stent, *Paradoxes of Free Will.* American Philosophical Society, DIANE, 2002. 284 pages. Pages 34 - 38. ISBN 0-87169-926-5

Jan Assmann, *Moses the Egyptian: The Memory of Egypt in Western Monotheism*.Harvard University Press, 1997. 288 pages. ISBN 0-674-58739-1

N. Shupak, *The Monotheism of Moses and the Monotheism of Akhenaten*. Sevivot, 1995.

William F. Albright, *From the Patriarchs to Moses II. Moses out of Egypt*. The Biblical Archaeologist, Vol. 36, No. 2 (May, 1973), pp. 48-76. doi 10.2307/3211050

Pantheism: A Non-Theistic Concept of Deity - Page 136, Michael P. Levine – 2002

A Feast for the Soul: Meditations on the Attributes of God: ... - Page x, Baháʾuʾlláh, Joyce Watanabe – 2006

Philosophy and Faith of Sikhism - Page ix, Kartar Singh Duggal – 1988

The Intellectual Devotional: Revive Your Mind, Complete Your Education, and Roam confidently with the cultured class, David S. Kidder, Noah D. Oppenheim, page 364

Raphael Lataster (2013). There was no Jesus, there is no God: A Scholarly Examination of the Scientific, Historical, and Philosophical Evidence & Arguments for Monotheism. p. 165. ISBN 1492234419. This one god could be of the deistic or pantheistic sort. Deism might be superior in explaining why God has seemingly left us to our own devices and pantheism could be the more logical option as it fits well with the ontological argument's 'maximally-great entity' and doesn't rely on unproven concepts about 'nothing' (as in 'creation out of nothing'). A mixture of the two, pandeism, could be the most likely God-concept of all.

Jump up to:*a b Alan H. Dawe (2011). The God Franchise: A Theory of Everything. p. 48.ISBN 0473201143. Pandeism: This is the belief that God created the universe, is now one with it, and so, is no longer a separate conscious entity. This is a combination of pantheism (God is identical to the universe) and deism (God created the universe and then withdrew Himself).*

Christianity and Other Religions, by John Hick and Brian Hebblethwaite. 1980. Page 178.

"'God' in Merriam-Webster (online)". Merriam-Webster, Inc. Retrieved2012-07-19.

The ulterior etymology is disputed. Apart from the unlikely hypothesis of adoption from a foreign tongue, the OTeut. "ghuba" implies as its preTeut-type either "*ghodho-m" or "*ghodto-m". The former does not appear to admit of explanation; but the latter would represent the neut. pple. of a root "gheu-". There are two Aryan roots of the required form ("*g,heu-" with palatal aspirate) one with meaning 'to invoke' (Skr. "hu") the other 'to pour, to offer sacrifice' (Skr "hu", Gr. χεηi;ν, OE "geotàn" Yete v).OED Compact Edition, G, p. 267

Barnhart, Robert K (1995). *The Barnhart Concise Dictionary of Etymology: The Origins of American English Words*, page 323. HarperCollins. ISBN 0-06-270084-7

Webster's New World Dictionary; "God n. ME < OE, akin to Ger gott, Goth guth, prob. < IE base * ĝhau-, to call out to, invoke > Sans havaté, (he) calls upon; 1. any of various beings conceived of as supernatural, immortal, and having special powers over the lives and affairs of people and the course of nature; deity, esp. a male deity: typically considered objects of worship; 2. an image that is worshiped; idol 3. a person or thing deified or excessively honored and admired; 4. [G-] in monotheistic religions, the creator and ruler of the universe, regarded as eternal, infinite, all-powerful, and all-knowing; Supreme Being; the Almighty"

Dictionary.com; "God /gɒd/ noun: 1. the one Supreme Being, the creator and ruler of the universe. 2. the Supreme Being considered with reference to a particular attribute. 3. (lowercase) one of several deities, esp. a male deity, presiding over some portion of worldly affairs. 4. (often lowercase) a supreme being according to some particular conception: The God of mercy. 5. Christian Science. the Supreme Being, understood as Life, Truth, Love, Mind, Soul, Spirit, Principle. 6. (lowercase) an image of a deity; an idol. 7. (lowercase) any deified person or object. 8. (often lowercase) Gods, Theater. 8a. the upper balcony in a theater. 8b. the spectators in this part of the balcony."

Barton, G.A. (2006). A Sketch of Semitic Origins: Social and Religious. Kessinger Publishing. ISBN 1-4286-1575-X.

"God". Islam: Empire of Faith. PBS. Retrieved 2010-12-18.

"Islam and Christianity", *Encyclopedia of Christianity* (2001): Arabic-speakingChristians and Jews also refer to God as *Allāh*.

L. Gardet. "Allah". Encyclopedia of Islam Online.

Hastings 2003, p. 540

Mattson MP. (2014) Superior pattern processing is the essence of the evolved human brain. Frontiers in Neuroscience 2014 Aug 22; 8:265

Froese, Paul; Christopher Bader (Fall–Winter 2004). "Does God Matter? A Social-Science Critique". Harvard Divinity Bulletin. 4 32. See Swami Bhaskar Ananda, *Essentials of Hinduism* (Viveka Press 2002) ISBN 1-884852-04-1

. *Sri Granth. Retrieved 2011-06-30.*

102. Quran 112:1–4

D. Gimaret. "Allah, Tawhid". Encyclopedia Britannica Online.

Robyn Lebron (2012). Searching for Spiritual Unity...Can There Be Common Ground? p. 117. ISBN 1-4627-1262-2.

Müller, Max. (1878) *Lectures on the Origin and Growth of Religion: As Illustrated by the Religions of India.* London: Longmans, Green and Co.

Smart, Jack; John Haldane (2003). Atheism and Theism. Blackwell Publishing. p. 8. ISBN 0-631-23259-1.

Lemos, Ramon M. (2001). A Neomedieval Essay in Philosophical Theology. Lexington Books. p. 34. ISBN 0-7391-0250-8.

"Philosophy of Religion.info – Glossary – Theism, Atheism, and Agnosticism". Philosophy of Religion.info. Archived from the original on 2008-04-24. Retrieved 2008-07-16.

"Theism – definition of theism by the Free Online Dictionary, Thesaurus and Encyclopedia". TheFreeDictionary.com. Retrieved 2008-07-16.

Sean F. Johnston (2009). The History of Science: A Beginner's Guide. p. 90. ISBN 1-85168-681-9. In its most abstract form, deism may not attempt to describe the characteristics of such a non-interventionist creator, or even that the universe is identical with God (a variant known as pandeism).

Paul Bradley (2011). This Strange Eventful History: A Philosophy of Meaning.
p. 156. ISBN 0875868762. Pandeism combines the concepts of Deism and Pantheism with a god who creates the universe and then becomes it.

Allan R. Fuller (2010). Thought: The Only Reality.
p. 79. ISBN 1608445909. Pandeism is another belief that states that God is identical to the universe, but God no longer exists in a way where He can be contacted; therefore, this theory can only be proven to exist by reason. Pandeism views the entire universe as being from God and now the universe is the entirety of God, but the universe at some point in time will fold back into one single being which is God Himself that created all. Pandeism raises the question as to why would God create a universe and then abandon it? As this relates to pantheism, it raises the question of how did the universe come about what is its aim and purpose?

Peter C. Rogers (2009). Ultimate Truth, Book 1. p. 121. ISBN 1438979681. As with Panentheism, Pantheism is derived from the Greek: 'pan'= all and 'theos' = God, it literally means "God is All" and "All is God." Pantheist purports that everything is part of an all-inclusive, indwelling, intangible God; or that the Universe, or nature, and God are the same. Further review helps to accentuate the idea that natural law, existence, and the Universe which is the sum total of all that is, was, and shall be, is represented in the theological principle of an abstract 'god' rather than an individual, creative Divine Being or Beings of any kind. This is the key element which distinguishes them from Panentheists and Pandeists. As such, although many religions may claim to hold Pantheistic elements, they are more commonly Panentheistic or Pandeistic in nature.

John Culp (2013). "Panentheism," *Stanford Encyclopedia of Philosophy*, Spring.

The Project Gutenberg EBook of *The Brothers Karamazov* by Fyodor Dostoyevsky pp259-261

Henry, Michel (2003). I am the Truth. Toward a philosophy of Christianity. Translated by Susan Emanuel. Stanford University Press. ISBN 0-8047-3780-0.

Edwards, Paul. "God and the philosophers" in Honderich, Ted. (ed)*The Oxford Companion to Philosophy*, Oxford University Press, 1995. ISBN=978-1 61592-446-2.

"A Plea for Atheism. By 'Iconoclast'", London, Austin & Co., 1876, p. 2.

Dawkins, Richard (2006). The God Delusion. Great Britain: Bantam Press. ISBN 0-618-68000-4

Dawkins, Richard (2006-10-23). "Why There Almost Certainly Is No God". The Huffington Post. Retrieved 2007-01-10.

Sagan, Carl (1996). The Demon Haunted World p.278. New York: Ballantine Books. ISBN 0-345-40946-9.

Stephen Hawking; Leonard Mlodinow (2010). The Grand Design. Bantam Books. p. 172. ISBN 978-0-553-80537-6.

Nikoletseas, Michael M. (2014). Deus Absconditus - The Hidden God. ISBN 978-1495336225.

Boyer, Pascal (2001). Religion Explained,. New York: Basic Books. pp. 142–243.ISBN 0-465-00696-5.

du Castel, Bertrand; Jurgensen, Timothy M. (2008). Computer Theology, Austin, Texas: Midori Press. pp. 221–222. ISBN 0-9801821-1-5.

Barrett, Justin (1996). "Conceptualizing a Non-natural Entity: Anthropomorphism in God Concepts" (PDF).

Rossano, Matt (2007). "Supernaturalizing Social Life: Religion and the Evolution of Human Cooperation" (PDF). Retrieved 2009-06-25.

Aquinas, Thomas (1990). Kreeft, Peter, ed. Summa of the Summa. Ignatius Press. p. 63.

Aquinas, Thomas (1990). Kreeft, Peter, ed. Summa of the Summa. Ignatius Press. pp. 65–69.

Aquinas, Thomas (1274). Summa Theologica. Part 1, Question 2, Article 3.

Curley, Edwin M. (1985). The Collected Works of Spinoza. Princeton University Press. ISBN 978-0-691-07222-7.

"Baruch Spinoza".

http://www.newadvent.org/summa/1002.htm#article 1

Summa of Theology I, q.2, The Five Ways Philosophers Have Proven God's Existence

Alister E. McGrath (2005). Dawkins' God: genes, memes, and the meaning of life. Wiley-Blackwell. ISBN 978-1-4051-2539-0.

Floyd H. Barackman (2001). Practical Christian Theology: Examining the Great Doctrines of the Faith. Kregel Academic. ISBN 978-0-8254-2380-2.

Gould, Stephen J. (1998). Leonardo's Mountain of Clams and the Diet of Worms. Jonathan Cape. p. 274. ISBN 0-224-05043-5.

The word *atheism* originated from the Greek ἄθεος (*atheos*), meaning "without god(s)".

Thomas Henry Huxley, an English biologist, was the first to come up with the word *agnostic* in 1869 *Dixon,*

*Thomas (2008). Science and Religion: A Very Short Introduction. Oxford: Oxford University Press. p. 63. ISBN 978-0-19-929551-7.*However, earlier authors and published works have promoted an agnostic points of view. They include Protagoras, a 5th-century BCE Greek philosopher. *"The Internet Encyclopedia of Philosophy - Protagoras (c. 490 - c. 420 BCE)". Archived from the original on 2008-10-14. Retrieved 2008-10-06. While the pious might wish to look to the gods to provide absolute moral guidance in the relativistic universe of the Sophistic Enlightenment, that certainty also was cast into doubt by philosophic and sophistic thinkers, who pointed out the absurdity and immorality of the conventional epic accounts of the gods. Protagoras' prose treatise about the gods began 'Concerning the gods, I have no means of knowing whether they exist or not or of what sort they may be. Many things prevent knowledge including the obscurity of the subject and the brevity of human life.'*

Francis Schüssler Fiorenza and Gordon D. Kaufman, "God", Ch 6, in Mark C. Taylor, ed, *Critical Terms for Religious Studies* (University of Chicago, 1998/2008), 136-140.

Gen. 17:1; 28:3; 35:11; Ex. 6:31; Ps. 91:1, 2

Gen. 14:19; Ps. 9:2; Dan. 7:18, 22, 25

Bentley, David (September 1999). The 99 Beautiful Names for God for All the People of the Book. William Carey Library. ISBN 0-87808-299-9.

Aquinas, Thomas (1274). Summa Theologica. Part 1, Question 3, Article 1

Augustine of Hippo (397). Confessions. Book 7.

Lang, David; Kreeft, Peter (2002). Why Matter Matters: Philosophical and Scriptural Reflections on the Sacraments. Chapter Five: Why Male Priests? Our Sunday Visitor. ISBN 978-1931709347.

Elaine H. Pagels "What Became of God the Mother? Conflicting Images of God in Early Christianity" Signs, Vol. 2, No. 2 (Winter, 1976), pp. 293-303

Coogan, Michael (October 2010). "6. Fire in Divine Loins: God's Wives in Myth and Metaphor". God and Sex. What the Bible Really Says (1st ed.). New York, Boston: Twelve. Hachette Book Group. p. 175. ISBN 978-0-446-54525-9. Retrieved2011-05-05. humans are modeled on elohim, specifically in their sexual differences.

"Human Nature and the Purpose of Existence". Patheos.com. Retrieved2011-01-29.

Quran 51:56

"Allah would replace you with a people who sin". islamtoday.net. Retrieved13 October 2013.

McGrath, Alister (2006). Christian Theology: An Introduction. Blackwell Publishing. p. 205. ISBN 1-4051-5360-1.

Plantinga, Alvin. "God, Arguments for the Existence of", *Routledge Encyclopedia of Philosophy*, Routledge, 2000.

Wierenga, Edward R. "Divine foreknowledge" in Audi, Robert. *The Cambridge Companion to Philosophy*. Cambridge University Press, 2001.

Beaty, Michael (1991). "God Among the Philosophers". The Christian Century. Retrieved 2007-02-20.

Pascal, Blaise. *Pensées*, 1669.

Nikoletseas, Michael M. (2014). Deus Absconditus - The Hidden God. ISBN 978-1495336225

Tuesday, December 8, 2009 (December 8, 2009). "More Americans Believe in Angels than Global Warming". Outsidethebeltway.com. Retrieved 2012-12-04.

Van, David (2008-09-18). "Guardian Angels Are Here, Say Most Americans". TIME. Retrieved 2012-12-04.

"Poll: Nearly 8 in 10 Americans believe in angels". CBS News. December 23, 2011. Retrieved 2012-12-04.

Salmon, Jacqueline L. "Most Americans Believe in Higher Power, Poll Finds". washingtonpost.com. Retrieved 2012-12-04.

Qur'an 15:27

ABOUT THE AUTHOR

Terry Hayes the retired school teacher, mentor, naval intelligence analyst and instructor has traveled the world asking the questions about God and religion. He is quick to tell you that GOD has no religion just man, but he will always tell you that you much respect everyone's right to practice that religion if this is what they want to do. Born and raised in Houston, Texas to two Baptist members he was told at an early age that you must always respect GOD. Being in the military gave him a chance to see man's religions up close and study what makes them so important.

Made in the USA
Middletown, DE
27 December 2024

68277095R00064